"MY SEDIMENTS, EXACTLY!"

"MY SEDIMENTS, EXACTLY!"

A Passionate Pilgrimage Through Wine and Life

Michael Andriaccio

&

(Joanne Castellani, Contributing Author)

"MY SEDIMENTS, EXACTLY!"

A Passionate Pilgrimage Through Wine and Life

I dedicate this to my lovely, extremely gifted and beautiful wife, Joanne, for being there every step of the way, and for leading me to steps that I would never have taken on my own.

ACKNOWLEDGMENTS

First, I want to thank my wonderful family for bringing me into a gene pool of longevity. I selected my parents well! They exposed me, from day one to all the good things in life, particularly food and the arts.

Nods go out to our myriad friends around the world who have opened countless doors into this incredible journey of music, art, literature, science, food, and wine.

Specifically, thanks to Dave Cosentino, a world-class restaurateur of the Trattoria Aroma establishments and Italian tour-director, for giving me the opportunity to be the wine educator at his numerous culinary enterprises, laying the groundwork for my ability to reach an audience.

To Frank and Nancy Grimaldi, proprietors of the famed San Marco Ristorante, for making every event special. As an aside, Frank is a classical guitar aficionado and a most competent player and collector of fine instruments. Frank and Nancy have hosted memorable Soirées with us and world-renowned artists just relaxing in their restaurant – conveniently, many guitars at hand!

A special thank you to Larry Draves and the late Meg Summersgill, great folks who hosted us in Bordeaux at the iconic Château Haut-Bailly.

And to Steve Siegel, Prof. Emeritus of the Niagara University College of Hospitality and Tourism, who engaged Joanne and me to guide them through the world of wine and olive oil.

Table of Contents

INTRODUCTION

Welcome to Michael's Cellar, where wine is food –
and a way of life. Have you ever thought about
societies where wine and olive oil are always present
on the dinner table? Did you ever wonder about
religions in which wine and oil are integral
components of their liturgies and rites? Isn't it
curious that people from societies where wine and
olive oil are dietary staples live to very old ages? It
all has to do with life and lifestyle. My lovely wife,
Joanne Castellani, and I love to eat. We are both of
Italian heritage and she is a Certified Olive Oil
Consultant. Every day, we enjoy wine and olive oil –

they are a part of our diet. Though wine will be the focus of this writing, later we will delve deeply into olive oil and its use as an ingredient and as a condiment.

A basic table: place settings, wine and olive oil.

For the past fifty years, I have been on a personal journey – a journey through the world of wine. I would like you to join me on this journey and along the way, I will acquaint you with this special world through its vocabulary, its history, its culture, its product and its place in society today. I will give you some insight into how wine is made and explore the many categories, types and styles of wine. We will also take a peek at the more popular regions and grape varieties. You will learn some simple techniques for selecting and serving wine and I will guide you, step by step, on how to taste wine and recognize what makes a great wine and what distinguishes it from lesser wines. Since experience is the best teacher, I will share with you some of my most memorable and defining wine encounters in the hope that you, too, will relate and be able to glean something that you can keep forever. To cap it all off, I'll show you how to build a cellar that is reflective of your individual tastes and more importantly, I will launch you on a lifelong journey through this fabulous, sensual and rewarding world of wine. Reading this book will forever change the way you think about wine.

To help you become familiar with the words and phrases in the vernacular of *"wine speak,"* I have presented them in a bold, italicized font.

PART 1

SEDIMENTAL JOURNEYS

The "new" *etiquette* of wine is not an etiquette of *pretense*. It is an etiquette predicated on *personal taste* – an etiquette that dispels some of the myths and pompous rites of the past while appreciating and fortifying age-old practices born from the idea that wine should be shown at its best. It is an etiquette defined by a *lifestyle*.

The journey for me has actually been a pilgrimage that has enriched my life to no end, for the world of wine is a world filled with wonderful, creative people, passionate people of various cultural backgrounds, and people with one bond that brings them all together – *WINE*. It's hard to imagine, but I have been drinking wine since I was four years old. That's right. I was born into an Italian family and at every meal, wine was present on the table. Not just wine, but olive oil, too. We never talked about it. It was just there like the bread, the vegetable side dish...just part of the meal. No one ever got drunk, or tipsy. We just had wine with every meal. I just took it for granted until a couple of experiences made me totally passionate about it and realized that it is truly something special on multiple levels.

Snack time!

Nothing could be more natural than this nectar of the gods. Think of yourself standing in a vineyard in front of a vine – it doesn't really matter what type of grapevine. At eye level, are the leaves that take in sunshine, wind, pollen, water in its many forms, insects and everything else. Underfoot are the soil, the mud, the rock through which the roots excavate and extract the minerals, the water, and the very character of the ground. Now, right in between at torso level, or the area that athletes would call the strike zone, are the grapes, those little berries that ripen under the sun, growing and filling with juice almost to the point of bursting from the sugar-intense liquid. At some point, the juice-heavy grape falls from the vine, hits the ground and the skin bursts, oozing that sweet juice onto the outer skin of the grape that is covered with that grey substance (*saccharomyces*) or simply, *yeasts*. The yeasts convert the sugar to alcohol and there you go. Wine is made – no human intervention needed!

No other substance on earth can break down barriers as effectively as wine. I will never forget, way back in 1981, Joanne and I took a wonderful trip to Stresa, a lovely, small town caressing the banks of Lago Maggiore in Italy's ultra-romantic Northern Lake region. The evening was notable. It was our 5th anniversary. To celebrate, we dined at a medieval seaside hotel and ordered a bottle of *Prosecco* to accompany dinner. This wine was no *Dom Pérignon*, but it had a simple *charm* about it. The *fruitiness*, the *texture* of the *bubbles* and the *nutty dryness* cajoled us to finish the whole bottle in short order. Twenty minutes after dinner, we found ourselves out in the piazza, attentively observing a boisterous Communist Party rally. For the record, Joanne and I are not Communists by any stretch, but we were taken by the nostalgic songs of the Motherland with our newfound Comrades!

Magari (Italian for...if only), our political leaders could take a page from this tome...who knows?

"In Vino Veritas"

"In wine there is truth." – Pliny the Elder

As I said, wine brings people together, and does so in a very special way. In short, wine makes friends. If you ever have an opportunity to visit the *Castello Banfi* in *Montalcino, Tuscany*, they offer a spectacular five-course lunch and wine tasting. On a recent trip to the region, Joanne and I, along with a couple of friends, were seated in the Castello's large, elegant, brick dining room on the top floor of the Castle. Each party in the room was seated at its own table. Naturally, in such circumstances, given the anticipation, the elegance, hints of formality and the fact that we were all strangers, there was no interaction whatsoever from one table to the next. Everyone was subdued, if not inhibited. By the time the third course was served with the third bottle of wine, we were all going to be Godparents to each other's children and well taken care of in each other's wills!

WINE IN OUR CULTURE

As far back as I can remember, I have always loved wine. Not just the wine, but everything about it, from its origins to the *corks* and *glasses* and certainly, the wine itself. Having been born and raised in the United States, I realize that this is a somewhat foreign and at times, taboo world. In this country (and others too), *alcohol* in its many forms has had many bad associations and connotations. It is often linked to the party life and has been used as a vehicle of escape or downright abuse. It is, in fact, a *controlled substance* in this country. There are many reasons for this, reasons that I need not delve into in this treatise. I mention it, however, because it's a vital point of departure when you look at wine and its place in society on a global level.

I am a second-generation Italian American. So wine is not as mysterious to me as it was to many of my childhood friends. I have been privileged to live a colorful life of Italianate origin that steered me into a lifelong career in the arts. As a child, I played in a basement that housed my grandfather's ancient *wine press* that is still enshrined in our wine cellar today. Once a year, that ominous, medieval device caused such a controlled commotion among family members that it was second only to the arrival of a cement truck.

As internationally touring concert artists, we have had the pleasure of being in so many parts of the world where life runs at a different pace from that which we are used to in the States. In Europe, where we have spent a considerable amount of time, there is one thing that you can count on. Mealtime is important. It is a time to recalibrate and recharge. In the States, mealtime is simply a speed bump – a necessary and brief interruption of whatever it is you are doing. In Europe, there is always wine at the table. The same is true for Central and South America, parts of the Middle East, parts of Asia, Africa and Australia. Only in recent years have Americans been awakened to the pleasures and benefits of wine and wine as a part of the meal.

Throughout history, wine has been associated with many religions and mythology as far back as records take us. The Bible has over five hundred references to wine all the way back to the Book of Genesis. The significance of wine at Passover is clearly defined in the Talmud and even in Iran. The storied, ancient city of Shiraz was the center of the region's wine trade, vines of which were brought to France during the Crusades. Art, music, literature, even science are hosts to ubiquitous references to figures such as Bacchus, Diogenes, and others. There are many reasons for this, not the least of which is dietary.

"Diogenes surly and proud...and unable to purchase a flask...he lived by the scent of his glass."

Audio track: *"Diogenes Surly and Proud"*, from the CD "An American Idyll"

(FDS 57924), Daniel McCabe, baritone with Michael Andriaccio, guitar.

YouTube link:

https://www.youtube.com/watch?v=Q0q2aQ9bzl0

WINE AND YOUR HEALTII

Bavarian youth enjoying Riesling after a band concert.

In many other cultures, wine is not a *controlled substance*. It is as much a part of *nutrition* and *diet* as any other *food*. One of the most astonishing observations that we made when we first began our travels was that we never saw anybody in a drunken or out-of-control state in a European restaurant. Another astonishing observation was that we watched these people sit at the table for hours on end, eating course after course of foods prepared with *olive oil*, accompanied by a glass of *mineral water* and a *glass of wine*. The kicker was that few of these people appeared to be overweight. Over the years, Joanne and I have tried to assimilate this diet into our daily routine. We have developed a real taste for *wine, water* and *olive oil*. These are our three beverages of preference. I consume nothing else but a single cup of coffee in the morning. That's it - wine (and water) with my meals and a small glass of wine (ca. 3 ounces) just before I go to bed. I drink it every day (discretely, of course, and never before driving) and my health and blood chemistry have improved over time. Aside from being *delicious*, it is *all-natural,* and full of *vitamins, minerals, flavonoids,* and *polyphenols* (including *peptides*) that have been proven to inhibit the growth of cancers, and delay dementia and Alzheimer's disease. It also has *antioxidants* that retard the aging process and *resveratrol* that works against heart disease.

Wine is a naturally mild *tranquilizer* and has been scientifically proven to aid in the *digestion of food* and the *control of cholesterol.* Studies have also revealed that frequent, consistent consumption of <u>small</u> amounts of wine is better than large amounts less frequently. It appears that the positive effect of wine on blood platelets doesn't last very long, maybe only a day or two, so it might be better to make it a small but consistent part of the diet. See *Wine Spectator* issue, December 2001. What I'm saying is that cultures that drink wine regularly also eat differently. Here goes that "lifestyle" thing again. We all know that Europeans drink wine regularly. We also know that they consume far more olive oil than Americans. Though Americans have increased their consumption of olive oil, the Mediterranean's have beaten us to it. Americans consume, per capita, one liter of olive oil per year, while the Italians, Greeks, and Spanish consume 13+ liters per person per year, according to the U.S. Department of Agriculture. Those are staggering statistics and speak volumes about the results of numerous health studies focusing on olive oil and wine. Forget the wine, look at the culture!

It is also important to know that salmonella cannot live very long in red wine (only seconds). That is why it is so important when dining out or in an unfamiliar venue, to have red wine with your meal.

I asked a French friend how much wine the average Frenchman drinks daily. Much to my surprise, he responded, "About a liter." This is what the "60 Minutes" documentary of 1991 defined as "*The French Paradox*" – fatty foods and wine for a healthy society. Obviously, these people are used to it. We are not. Check with your doctor in case you have any restrictions or are on medications, and again, never drink before driving or operating machinery.

Wine consumption in Europe has drastically changed in the last twenty years. Yes, the adults, who are the traditional wine drinkers, are still consuming the same amount, ca. 750 ml to 1,000 ml a day, <u>always</u> with food, but the millennials and Gen Z have changed the dynamic. These young folks are drinking lattes, sodas, spirit-spiced juices and beers instead of wine. Sound familiar? Thank you, internet and globalization!

Extra virgin olive oil, as I pointed out, is another nectar of the gods and garnishes our vegetables. It is used as a base for marinades and in place of butter. Since Joanne and I have assimilated this diet, our annual blood tests have confirmed that our health has been improving. Our HDL levels are off the charts on the high end, our LDL is low and our triglycerides are off the charts on the low end. The quotidian "anointing" of one's digestive system aids in all metabolic processes. It has even been found that when wine is consumed with food, significantly less alcohol is absorbed by the body than when it is consumed without food, up to two-thirds less! This diet, along with a generally healthy lifestyle, is what I believe keeps the Europeans fit. Instead of driving everywhere (though, I must admit that we are having a bad influence on them in this regard), they walk after every meal and their foods suffer less of the *"processing"* that our foods undergo here. Their refrigerators are much smaller than ours, compelling them to buy more FRESH food several times a week. So, you ask, what does this have to do with wine? EVERYTHING, I say.

Recent research from Rutgers University and Hunter College scientists shows that an ingredient in extra virgin olive oil, *oleocanthal*, actually kills certain types of cancer cells without any harm to healthy cells. It apparently targets specific proteins in the cancer cells, causing them to break down and die. (See *Molecular and Cellular Oncology,* by LeGendre, Foster and Breslin)

DEVELOPING A PERSONAL TASTE

Like anything else, our first experience with something is what we tend to remember most. The things that we are "used to" are the things that become the "standard" for all of our future experiences, and wine is no exception. Developing a *"wine memory"* is critically important in establishing a reliable platform from which to proceed. I was a nut when I was young – many believe that I still am today, but that's a topic for someone else to write about. Back then, I would go into a wine shop with Joanne and spend hours just walking up and down the aisles awestruck, looking reverently at each of those exotic bottles from places in the world where I felt that I needed to be. After reading a small book about Bordeaux (I can't even find the book now or remember the title), I went to the wine shop and came upon a bottle of 1975 *Château d'Agassac, Ludon Medoc, Cru Bourgeois*. It was the label that attracted me. The bottle was $4.99 and a real stretch for me at the time. I will never forget how I brought that bottle home, gingerly set it on the table as if it were a bottle of nitroglycerin, and just kept staring at it. I was hypnotized by the presence of a thoroughbred *Bordeaux* in our kitchen.

The next conflict within me was this. I wanted to taste it, but I also wanted to keep it forever. This dilemma was to be my companion for the rest of my life. *"I want to drink this wine. But I want to keep it in my cellar! But I should drink it – at least taste it. But no, I should keep it in the cellar to improve for the next 15 years."* (I'll speak more about this later.) Well, being so fortunate to have Joanne as my Greek chorus, she quietly said, "Let's just drink it. Isn't that why you bought it?" "OK!" So, we planned a special meal for this Holy of Holy beverage. I stood the bottle upright, undisturbed, in the dining room two days ahead of time. For two days, I lustfully stared at that bottle standing so provocatively on our table. It was no secret that that bottle had cast its spell upon me. It would not stop seducing me. An hour before dinner, I gently caressed the bottle and without moving it, I carefully placed the corkscrew, then inserted it and slowly began withdrawing the cork, one careful, rhythmic turn after another. I remember thinking, "Oh my God! I've never seen a cork this long before!" It was obvious from the moment I opened it, that it was having its way with me and I recklessly surrendered. When the firm, moist cork was fully withdrawn, I let out a sigh and curiously but carefully examined it. It was almost time to light a cigarette, if you know what I mean! I saw the Château name, vintage and logo burnished onto that cork. I had never seen that before either. FYI, Bordeaux corks traditionally have been a bit longer than most others.

Then, I proceeded to decant the wine, candle and the whole nine yards. Let me remind you that this was a $5.00 bottle of wine, a 1975 being consumed in 1979. I will never forget the smell of this wine when the cork was removed, nor will I ever forget the color of the wine in the decanter. The room began to fill with the seductive yet sacred scent of this wine. When it was poured into the crystal wine glasses, the color was even more intense, and the bouquet was nothing like I had experienced before. When I slowly brought the glass to the edge of my lips and the first drop hit the tip of my tongue, this tiny drop exploded into an array of flavors and sensations that I can still taste right now. The insides of my cheeks by my jaw began to pucker and flavor after flavor unfolded. Every sip thereafter was different from the previous one and the interaction with the various food flavors was again, nothing that I had ever experienced before. I was hooked. That was the defining moment, my rightful passage into the world of wine.

Now after fifty years, the love affair continues, but like any successful relationship, you must keep working at it. Please remember that this was a relatively inexpensive wine at the time, but I was lucky. Château d'Agassac is a pedigree Bordeaux with a decades-long heritage of being one of the real values and consistent performers of "classic-style" Bordeaux. It is not so readily available in the States anymore, but I understand that it is very popular in the Scandinavian countries at the moment.

What does this story have to do with the topic? Well, this style of wine has become my standard for Bordeaux and a type of wine that I have built my entire wine cellar around. Somehow, I found a way to buy a case of the 1975, then later, two cases of the 1976 and years later, three cases of the 1978. I'm sorry to say that they are all gone, but what wonderful evenings they brought to the table! Every wine I taste today somehow relates to that first 1975 Bordeaux I had years ago.

Pretense is out. Personal taste is in.

In order to start developing your personal taste for wine, go to a wine shop and buy ten different reds, and five different whites. Not all at the same time. You don't have to spend more than $12.00 a bottle to find a type or "style" of wine that you really like.

Nor should you feel that you must limit yourself to a single, particular *style*. Just remember that when you taste one you like, take *notes* so that you have a platform from which you can make comparisons. I guarantee that you too, will meet that defining moment in your life with wine. Here are some eminently *drinkable* and *approachable* wines that will be clearly *distinctive* so that you can better focus on the direction that you wish to pursue. For the reds, I would suggest a California *Cabernet Sauvignon*, a *Merlot* from Washington State or Oregon, an Australian *Shiraz*, a *Chianti Classico* (Tuscany-Italy), a *Barbaresco* (N. Italy), a *Medoc* (*Bordeaux*, France, but don't try a *Saint-Émilion* or *Graves* yet; they are merlot-based Bordeaux). Also, try a California *Zinfandel* (stay away from white zinfandel!), a *Burgundy* (*pinot noir*), a *Rioja* (Spain), a *Côtes du Rhône* (S. France) and a *Beaujolais-Villages* (Burgundy region).

For the whites, I would recommend a California *Chardonnay*, a California *Sauvignon Blanc*, a *Pinot Grigio* (Tuscany-Italy), a French Chardonnay and a *Frascati* (Italy).

These wines are all vastly different. If you were to compare them at one tasting, the differences would be most obvious, but they are so diverse in *taste* and *style* that you will still be able to make your personal observations with credulity and confidence when sipped at different times.

Good wine or great wine?

It is a big *misconception* that one has to spend a great deal of money to obtain a good bottle of wine. First of all, you shouldn't have GREAT wine every day. GOOD wine every day makes the GREAT ones all the more special. Even at the great *Châteaux*, they drink "*everyday*" wines and only revert to the cellars for special occasions. Most everyday wines can be acquired in a price range from $10.00 to $15.00. Like anything else, though, some poor wines may be priced at the high end and some very good wines may be priced at the low end. There are many reasons for this but that is not for us to deal with. All you need to know is that you should look around, do a little homework, be adventuresome and make friends with your supplier. I find this to be the most fun of all. All you should be looking for is what I call a *wine of integrity*. Now that you have an idea of what makes me tick and the direction that I'm headed, let's advance to the specific topics themselves.

Who invented wine?

I touched on this earlier but let's review. Do you know that no human intervention is requisite in the production of wine? That's right! Wine will happen with or without us. Now let's get right to it. You can see for yourself how it happens. First, go to your grocery store and buy a bunch of red grapes (white will work but red makes the experiment more obvious). Carefully remove a grape from the *cluster*, handle it carefully and try to keep the *stem* on it. Do you see the white, chalky substance on the skin near the stem? That white matter is a collection of natural *yeasts* – a cocktail of *bacteria* known as *saccharomyces*. Now, gently squeeze the grape from the bottom with pressure pushing towards the stem. As the *skin* pops open and *juice* oozes out (notice that the juice is not red), the juice will come into contact with the white matter on the skin. Voilà, *fermentation* begins, the *yeasts* convert the *sugar* to *alcohol* and wine is made. Can it be simpler? Can the process be any more natural?

Ripe grapes

with

saccharomyce

As simple as the process is, the real beauty is the *"art"* of making wine. This is where the unity of *humans, soil, climate* and *vine* has evolved into a *creative process*. No two people, no two vineyards will produce the very same wine. It's impossible. There are too many variables. The *soil,* the *climate,* the *altitude,* the *latitude* and *exposure* of the *land* as well as *drainage, type, age* and *care of the vine,* all impact the final product. So do the *training of the vines,* the *time of harvest,* the *handling of the grapes,* the *crushing,* the *fermenting* and *racking* processes, *temperature control, timing, aging* and *container material,* all affect the wine. Many wines are *"blended"* relegating to the *winemaker* the tremendous individuality that is so evident in many wines. Some wines can be "crafted" including many whites. In fact, it is often said that red wines are made in the vineyard and white wines are made in the winery.

WINE AND FOOD

Do wines and foods from the same culture –

even region – really complement one another?

There is something to be said for the natural order of life. Life like art, maintains a certain *"stylistic consistency"* that lends *rhythm* and *architecture* to hold it all together. Indigenous *wildflowers* and *herbs*, characteristics of the *soil* and *climate* (*terroir*) are essential elements of food and wine. Foods and grapes that share the same habitat as their winegrower/maker or chef are married to each other. Joanne brought a bottle of *Laudemio, extra virgin olive oil, first cold press* home from Florence one year. This spectacular olive oil is produced on the fabled *Antinori Estate*. The *Antinori* family is one of the ancient, premier banking, *wine* and *oil* producers in *Tuscany*. We hosted an Italian wine tasting one evening and between the appetizer and the primo, we had a tasting of the Laudemio accompanied by the '97 *Antinori Badia a Passignano Chianti Classico*. If the *nose* of each didn't betray the fact that they were related, the *taste* and *texture* were a slap on the side of the head. The *consistency of style*, and *peripheral nuances* were hardly subtle. Even some novice guests were blown away. For a similar experiment, if the Laudemio is not available, *Badia a Coltibuono* extra virgin olive oil seems to be a bit more readily available here. Try it with the *Badia a Coltibuono Chianti Classico Riserva.*

Pizze Napolitane

Le pizze (the pizzas) shown here are a culinary treat from Sorrento. Remember *terroir*? The perfect wine for these is *Aglianico* from that region (*Campania*). The ingredients and grapes were all grown in the rich, volcanic soil at the foot of Mt. Vesuvius. It is truly difficult to not notice this when dining there.

Does it make sense to have a cocktail before dinner or a tasting?

No. Does this mean that you shouldn't? Not at all. You just have to realize that you won't get the most out of the wine that you drink afterward. Cocktails, because of the high levels of *alcohol, sugar* and various other *exotic tastes* present in them, will *neutralize* certain components of the wine and completely alter the tastebuds' ability to discern other subtle elements of the wine as well as the food. My experience is that those individuals who indulge in a cocktail (or two) prior to an evening of wine usually wake up the next morning with a bad headache and then blame it on the wine. They usually say that they can't tolerate sulfites and the wine served, had too many. Make no mistake, sulfites are a byproduct of the fermentation process in all wines. I guess you must ask yourself what your objective is. I certainly would not encourage a cocktail before a rare or even moderately expensive bottle of wine.

If you wish to have something to relax you and stimulate the taste buds and digestive system, try a glass of *dry vermouth* (white) on the rocks. It's very *fragrant, flavorful* and *dry*, acting as more of an *appetite "stimulant"* rather than a *suppressant.* Even a *Campari* will function nicely as an aperitif. If there are munchies around before dinner, say nuts or olives, there are no better accompaniments for these than *dry fino sherry* or *Prosecco.* After this combo, I am always ravished and can't wait to get to the table for the first sip of wine.

What wine with what food?

This is where whimsy and personal taste rule. You can be very creative here and still experience unforgettable combinations of food and wine. Old myths generally work but pale next to the excitement created by new cuisine and the introduction of stunningly new wines and wine styles. If the wines and foods don't happen to work together, you at least want to make certain that they don't fight each other. In order to understand and appreciate this concept, it is important for you to experience both ends of the spectrum. Try a sip of red *Bordeaux* after a bite of flounder or cod without any condiments. Ughhhhh! It's like eating a steel bar. Then, try a sip of *Napa Valley Cabernet Sauvignon* after a taste of filet mignon. This simple experiment will last you a lifetime. I am privileged to have had uncountable celestial taste combinations, the most memorable being a 1973 *Santa Sofia Amarone* (consumed in 1998). I went to our local cheese purveyor and told her about the wine. She pulled out a well-aged, high-end *gorgonzola*. At this moment, as I am writing this, I can actually taste it and tell you who was seated at what place at the table and what they were wearing. It was that remarkable a moment.

Typically, in most cultures, the best cuisine is the simplest, derived from quality ingredients readily at hand. Recipes are not really "recipes" but improvisations with an aleatory selection of good things that happen to be at hand. In Rome, it is referred to as, *"La Cucina Povera"* or the poor kitchen or cuisine.

Simple...olive oil, onions, mushrooms, spinach, peppers

Just add eggs and your favorite wine.

*Red
with
meat
-
White
with
fish?*

*There are reds AND whites that
can work well with both*

This will work if you are eating a hunk of ungarnished meat and a slab of baked, unseasoned fish. However, this is not life in today's kitchen. Just look at the pics above. It is obvious that this adage has some merit. If you have mild meat, such as pork loin served with a light, creamy glaze, a *Napa Valley Zinfandel* could make you forget that there's food on the plate. On the other hand, blackened tuna steak would absolutely devastate a *sauvignon blanc* or *pinot grigio*. So what do you do? Look at the overall *impact* of the dish and select a wine that you like that has a comparable impact, regardless of what anyone tells you. Again, pretense is out and personal taste is "in". There are few more enjoyable culinary moments than those impromptu occasions when you are with good friends and grab a bottle of your favorite wine and serve it with some of your favorite "fast" food. During Monday Night Football, a $15.00 bottle of *Napa Zinfandel* is a great company to a salami sub dressed in olive oil. A

$10.00 *Vin de Pays d'Oc* is all you need for a cheeseburger, while a $10.00 *sauvignon blanc* yearns for a turkey or ham club sandwich.

Even a novice, however, will notice the imbalance posed by an everyday meal accompanied by a very noble wine and a gourmet meal with a vin ordinaire. It is so striking. Not long ago, Joanne and I were privileged to share a few dining experiences with New York Times acclaimed cook and author, Marlene (Chou-Chou) de Blasi at her home in Orvieto, Italy. She is real big on the origins of great taste combinations as far back as medieval times. One pair in particular was the sweet/salt phenomenon as in prosciutto and melon. In this instance, an *Antinori '98 Campogrande, Orvieto Classico Bianco* was the perfect choice, but back to the point. One night, not being aware of her menu, I brought an *Avignonesi, '93 Vino Nobile di Montepulciano Riserva*. She had prepared a basic but delicious brodo followed by a simple linguini dish. It was not a match. The wine, in her words, was "far too noble for the meal". Two nights later, the opposite proved to be true. So, try to match, at least the quality of the wine with the quality of the food. A *Château Margaux* or an *Angelo Gaja* won't work with sandwiches any better than a *Bardolino* with Fois Gras and Bouef Bourguignon. Just remember that basically, your favorite wine with your favorite food is almost always a match if the impact is balanced.

Is the elegant sorbet a real palate cleanser?

In my humble opinion, no. In fact, I think it alters the taste of subsequent wines and foods. It appears to be mostly a ceremonial item – an accessory to give the impression that the establishment is high-brow. The sorbet that is usually served is much too sweet to be positioned between a first and second, or even a third course. It makes subsequent wines and foods taste flat. In reality, all that is needed to cleanse the palate is a bite of fresh bread without seeds and a sip of water, or better yet, sparkling water.

PART 2

THE SENSUAL SIPPER

TASTING THE WINE

We have all heard unbelievable stories about people who could blindly sip some wine and tell you what wine it is and from what *vintage*. In fact, while we were at the *Castello Banfi* in *Montalcino, Tuscany*, one of the servers informed us that they had just hired a young, *"virtuoso" taster* from Japan who possessed a virtually infallible palate with a repertoire at the time of over two thousand different wines! Truly, this is quite astonishing and most enviable, but frankly, I don't think that I want that kind of pressure from something I enjoy so much. I just want to *appreciate* it at every level. It can be as *simple* or *complex* as I want it to be. The Europeans know how to do it at every level. In fact, they know how to appreciate <u>everything</u> in life at every level and we can learn a great deal from them.

A perfect example of what I mean by "every level" is an experience we had on a recent trip to France. We were in the *Rhône* area, Cannes la Bocca to be precise. We walked into a tiny, family-run restaurant – so intimate that half of the family was seated at tables talking to the rest of the family members who were cooking in the "kitchen" which was a tiny space behind a counter. The cook, the mother (how unusual), was taking our order from behind the stove as we sat at our table a few feet away. She put our rack of lamb on a roaster in front of us and while it was cooking, she presented us with the *"wine list"* – a single bottle of *Vacqueyras*, a very good table wine from the region that she had "selected". No other wine could have been more suited to the occasion – it was simply a wonderful delight and went perfectly with the meal. In contrast, we stopped in Paris on our return home and walked into an elegant, typically Parisian brasserie. The archetypically aloof Parisian waiter presented us with the menu and wine list. We ordered Filet au Poivre au Jus (Filet Mignon with black pepper sauce). The moment I ordered the wine, it was an apocalyptic – a turning point. The waiter became our very best friend on earth and could not do enough for us the rest of the evening. I guess that we had established our credibility by selecting a young *Listrac Medoc* with the meal. The match was *balanced, complementary* and *delicious – perfect*. He even brought us cognac "on the house" after dinner and begged for our return! Lesson? The most effective way to disarm a French waiter is to order the right wine! The broader lesson? When in Rome

...

The whole point is that if you know a little bit – the right little bit about wine, your enjoyment goes much further than the glass. It extends to your everyday life. It does NOT mean that when offered a glass of wine that you should be critical or feel that you HAVE TO say something profound about it. In fact, I am quite weary of all of the tired words used over and over again to describe wine. We all know that it tastes like cherries or currants. Have you ever heard anyone say that it tastes like grapes? I haven't and that is most surprising to me. A REAL *wine connoisseur* just appreciates the fact that he or she is enjoying a glass of wine at the moment. The occasion requires nothing else other than to enjoy it. That's it! In order to help you get to this point, I have drawn upon fifty years of my personal experience in *tasting* and *collecting* wine, to put in place a very simple procedure that assists me in getting the most out of the wines that I drink. Now, I would like to share this with you. Let us begin.

When someone is passionate about something, they are in fact, "*sensual*" about it. They try to flood their senses with whatever it is that excites them... *ALL* their senses. After all, each of our senses speaks to us in many different yet unique ways. Not until you have indulged ALL your available senses when tasting wine, will you be able to grasp just what it is that you're drinking. Wines are distinctive in the manner in which they flood your senses. If you have a little bit of background, highly developed senses and some clues as to what to look for, the outer reaches of ecstasy are limitless!

Let's explore these senses one by one, but before we do, let's make sure that we have everything we need. First, we need an instrument – the instrument, in this case, is the *wine glass*. The glass is not just the container. It is the instrument that feeds our senses in order to appreciate the wine. There are five equally important parts to the instrument or glass: the base, the stem, the bowl, the chimney and the rim. The base allows the glass to stand securely on a flat surface. The stem is the "handle" that allows for secure handling and swirling. Swirling aerates the wine, releasing its aroma and bouquet. NB. Despite what you see, even from many pros in the wine business, fingers should NEVER EVER touch any part of the glass higher than the stem. Fingerprints obscure the beautiful, visual quality of the wine as shards of light enter the glass from all directions. The visual quality of the wine is not only a sight to behold, it tells a great deal about the wine even before we sip it. Secondly, wine is a delicate and fragile chemical compound and alcohol, a vital component, evaporate at 65° F. Heat from your hand will change the character and body of the wine.

The bowl holds the wine. We fill the glass ONLY to the widest part of the bowl to provide maximum aeration and surface exposure to air. The chimney or part from the widest point of the bowl to the rim concentrates the fumes as they rise to the rim for the most luxurious olfactory experience and then the rim guides the wine through our lips. There are many different types of wine glasses and we will explore them later.

There is a very useful and important term that we must embrace. Have you ever heard the word "terroir"? *Terroir* (pronounced tayr-waar') is ostensibly one of those esoteric terms that Robert Mondavi refers to as *"wine speak"*. Have you ever experienced a taste or smell that immediately transported you to a faraway time, event or place that you know very well – a place or event that is a real part of you, like the warm smell of Grandma's cooking, perhaps? It actually recreates the experience of being there. *Terroir* is the character of a wine that is synthesized by the particular *soil* and *climate* of its place of origin and it is distinctive in every good wine, i.e., wine that has not been altered or "manipulated" by excessive *filtration* or other *neutralizing* techniques. It is the Tuscan sun, cypress and olive trees with tastes of earth and the sometimes *"rustic"* feel of a *Vino Nobile di Montepulciano*. I swear that every time I have a sip of this wonderful wine, I am once again standing in the Pallazzo that houses the offices of *Le Cantine Avignonesi,* overlooking the Tuscan landscape from the fortressed walls of that glorious medieval town. Terroir is a very important word in the characterization of wine. Let us now embark on a sensual journey.

SIGHT

This process comes into play far sooner than you might think. It does NOT begin in the *glass*. It begins in the *wine shop*. Look at the *bottle shapes* and *labels,* for they tell you a great deal about the wine. As a general rule, straight, tall, severely rounded *shoulders* near the top suggest a *Bordeaux* style wine. A wider bottle with a slightly rounded shoulder that begins two-thirds up the bottle may indicate a *Burgundy* style wine and a tall, narrow bottle with a gradually sloping shoulder is usually a *German* type wine. Now, with all of the trendy marketing ploys out there today, this is only a general rule at best.

Bordeaux style, Burgundy style, German style.

The bottle shapes are not arbitrary or simply traditional. Their shapes have a purpose. The Bordeaux style has severe shoulders to impede the flow of sediment into the glass. Keep in mind that Bordeaux wines are primarily cabernet sauvignon and merlot-based reds that often produce a heavy, unpleasant sediment over time. The graceful, longer shoulders of the Burgundy bottle are so formed because the sediment thrown by the principal grape, pinot noir, is finer and inert to the wine, and is not really an issue when pouring. That is why decanting burgundies is often not necessary. This also applied to *Nebbiolo* based wines that are very similar in personality to pinot noir. The German or Alsatian bottles need not pay any attention to sediment. Yes, there are many exceptions.

Not long ago, Joanne and I were in Manhattan, and we stopped to have dinner at one of our favorite steak houses, Ben Benson's on West 52nd Street. We were seated at a booth in the rear and right next to us was an empty booth. Two waiters approached the empty booth and set the table with REAL wine glasses and two *Riedel decanters*. This caught my interest immediately. Next, I saw a waiter with two bottles of very distinguishable shapes and colors. I turned to Joanne and said, "Hey, babe, catch what's going on over there! That guy's opening two *Angelo Gaja Barbarescos* and *decanting* them, and the guests aren't even here yet!" Now, the bottles were twelve feet away, but I knew those bottles. These are some expensive wines – in a wine shop, they go for as much as $300.00 a bottle, but THIS was in a New York restaurant. THIS was a BIG DEAL – a wine tab alone of about $1,200.00. I summoned the waiter and said, "WOW! Those are *Gaja's* you're pouring!" His response was, "How did YOU know? By the bottles?" "Of course," I replied and gave him my card. Once again, the waiter could not do enough for us the rest of the night. That event was apparently a ritual in that establishment. A very successful stockbroker would reserve a table for a fine wine tasting every few weeks and this was his drill. Not too shabby.

Essentially, there are two *categories* of wine: *varietal* named after the *grape variety*) and *regional* (named after the *region of origin*). There are some important and recognizable exceptions. Some good examples of popular *varietals* are *cabernet sauvignon, chardonnay* and *merlot*. Some *regional* examples would be *Beaujolais, Rioja, Chablis, Champagne, Barolo,* etc.

A good look at the *label* will tell you what the wine is (the grape variety) or where it is from or both, the *vintage* if any, the level of *alcohol* and the volume. It will also tell you a very important piece of information, the *producer*. Some are better than others. Look for legal *designations* such as *A.O.C. (Appellation d'Origine Controllée* in France) or *D.O.C.G. (Denominazione d'Origine Controllata e Guarantita* in Italy). These are strict government designations for grapes grown and wines produced in specifically *classified regions* and by *regulated methods*. It is a mark of security to know the origin of what's inside the bottle. The word *"reserve"* or *"riserva"* means *aged in oak* for up to two years prior to bottling. *Reserve* wines from a great *vintage* generally keep very long due to the high extraction of *tannin* from the oak *barriques, botti* or *barrels*. In *Spanish* wines, look for the words *"Riserva"* or *"Crianza"*.

Of course, the German wines have a history of controls and categorizations from *Deutscher Wein* to *Prädikatzwein* defining the regions. But they go even further to describe the ripeness of the fruit, i.e., from *Kabinett* to *Trokenbeerenauslese*.

In the USA, we have evolved over time to identify *AVAs* or *American Viticultural Areas*, not always indicated on the labels. For example, California alone has over one hundred and forty AVAs. Some of the most common are Rutherford, Howell Mountain and Mt. Veeder in Napa Valley and Dry

Creek, Sonoma Valley and Los Carneros in Sonoma County.

Now, you're back home from the shop, and assuming that you bought a bottle or two, it's time to <u>TRY</u> some. The item we must visually examine is the *seal* or *capsule* around the *cork* and *neck*. Why is this important? Because wine's best friend in the glass is its worst enemy in the bottle – *AIR!* Is the seal intact? If not, this is probably not a problem unless there are tears with brown, black or deep red, goopy matter inside. This is a sign of a bad cork or that the bottle was "*oozing*" or "*leaking*". This could be a problem but, in many cases, you can get lucky and still have a wonderful wine inside. Assuming that you have a pristine seal, remove it with a *foil cutter* and look at the top of the cork for the same signs of "*foreign matter*". Gently extract the cork and look at it closely. Is it *firm*? Does it show signs of *oozing*? Is it *moldy*? Does it have *crystals* on the bottom? Does it have a bad odor?

About a year or so after I really "got into" wine, I purchased a bottle of *Mâcon Villages*, a *chardonnay-based* wine from *Burgundy* (*regional* wine). We had planned a special meal around this bottle. When I opened it, I looked at the bottom of the cork and saw a whole collection of clear crystals. "Oh, no!" I exclaimed. "This bottle went bad!" And I proceeded to empty the entire contents down the drain. It was only a few days later that I learned how utterly ignorant and stupid I had been. Those crystals, which by the way, are inert to the wine, are potassium nitrite and are a sign of a very well-made white wine! Well, back to the point, all of these elements are clues as to what's to come. After wiping the top of the open bottle to remove any *mold, bacteria* or anything else that can cause "*off*" odors or tastes, pour some wine into a glass. A plain, white tablecloth is helpful here.

When poured into the glass, look at the wine. Hold it up to the light! What is the *color*? What is the *color* like? How intense is the *color*? Now is the time that the glass is raised for *sipping*. Remember, don't grab the glass by the *bowl*! Now, I'm not trying to make you behave in a pretentious manner or make a *"wine snob"* out of you, but there is a good reason to use the *stem*. One of the most beautiful and telling characteristics of a wine is the *color*. A greasy glass with fingerprints is not very attractive and does nothing to flatter the *appearance* of the wine or enhance the *overall experience*. Secondly, as I noted earlier, your body heat changes the *temperature* of the wine and causes it to react differently to the air around it. Back to the point – is it *clear* or *cloudy*? Is it *deep* or *light*? Is the color *consistent* all around the glass or are there *"brown edges*"? (This is typical of a *mature* wine.) Is there any *sediment* in the glass? (*Sediment* is a result of either little or no *filtration*, or *tannins* bonding with other elements in the wine to form large molecules that precipitate over the years to the bottom of the glass, bottle or decanter.) Is the wine *opaque* or *translucent*? Does the shade of red, for example, resemble anything to you (*cherries*, *blackcurrants*, etc.)? How does the wine *cling* to the inside of the glass when *swirled*? Does it have long, wide *legs*, or is it runny? The "*legs*" are the long, gothically arching drip streams that cling to the glass after the wine has been swirled. The height, distance between them, thickness and time required for them to develop are determined by the amount of *glycerol* in the wine. Generally, the less *glycerol* in the wine, the runnier it is and vice versa. A well-made and developed wine with a good *structure* will have great *legs* and a firm *body*, since *glycerol* is a creation of the fermentation process. This is a clue as to how it may *"feel"* in your mouth. The way it clings to the glass is the way it will cling to your mouth.

Swirling will tell you about the *glycerol* content and possibly the *texture* of the wine in the mouth. The *intensity* of each of these attributes is also a characteristic of each type of wine. So, the more you can recognize the various characteristics, the greater your success in identifying types and styles of wine in *blind tastings*. Each grape variety brings a different *color, clarity* and *body* to each wine.

In review, look at the wine. What color is it – red or white? Is it *still* or *sparkling*? (Sparkling wine is so named because of the *bubbles* that are caused by a *second fermentation* in the bottle.) Since you already know if you bought a varietal or a regional wine, the answers to these two questions already make you look like Alexis Lichine. You can identify four types of wine and you haven't even tasted one yet! See! You are on your way!

SMELL

What a <u>sense</u>! Sometimes, I wish I were a bloodhound! There are some *odors*, *fragrances*, *scents* that you just can't forget. Often, just thinking about the circumstance and you can conjure the fragrance on the spot. Joanne and I were once on a bus from Madrid to Granada. I was awakened from a deep sleep by the most amazing smell – a very strong but wonderful fragrance. We were passing through a tiny, Andalucian mountain town, all pure white buildings staged against parched, brown earth and a brilliant blue sky, a village surrounded by olive trees as far as you could see in any direction. All you could smell were green olives. At any second, I can close my eyes and I am right there. Similar, intense, *olfactory images* are common and should be encouraged to be a regular part of the wine experience. Don't just *smell* or *taste* – get into the moment and remember it.

For me, this part of the tasting procedure is the "big tease". This is the *approach* – the sense of wonder, mystery, anticipation, even hope in some cases as you begin the process of *"internalizing"* the wine.

Bring the glass to your nose. No!!!! Don't swirl it yet! Be patient! Take a healthy *sniff* from the center of the glass. Go ahead, don't be bashful, put your nose right inside the glass. *Remember* the *sensation*. What does it *smell* like? What do you smell? Does it smell like *flowers, fruit, chemicals* or all of the above? Maybe there is no smell at all. Withdraw your nose and *think* about it while your *olfactory* senses are *remembering, recovering* and *regrouping*. Does the sensation *evolve* at all? Let's go back to sight. Now, rigorously swirl the wine in the glass so that it covers virtually the entire inside of the glass. This technique exposes the wine to air and will enhance all of the *flavor* and *scent* components of the wine. This is called *"volatilizing the esters"*. (It is also the best time to visually check out the *glycerol* by looking closely at the *legs*.)

It is now time to take another healthy *sniff*. You should have a more *intense* and *diversified* experience. The sniffing is critically important for it introduces the wine to your *palate* through your *sinuses*. It is a marvelous sensation and a very accurate clue as to what is to come. What do you *smell*? Is it *wood, fruit, alcohol, wildflowers, spices, smoke, tobacco, leather* – *perhaps lead pencil shavings*? Can you savor the *"aroma"* (the actual *fragrance* of the grape) or the *"bouquet"* (combination of grape fragrance and all of the other more complex scents such as cedar, flowers, etc.)? Perhaps upon sight, it was very intense and inviting, but there is no *"nose"*. You can't really smell anything. This is not necessarily a bad thing. The wine may just need more time to *breathe*. Some fine wines from average vintages taste wonderful but have little or no nose. This is the advantage of *decanting* a wine before serving it. It enables the wine to *"oxidize"* more rapidly and efficiently. Can you detect any sense of *terroir* from the smell? Is it *earthy, rustic, refined, elegant*?

There are some wines that can't wait to share their goods with you. In rare instances, you don't even need to go through all of this. One night, we opened a 1978 *Château Lascombes*, not a great vintage, but within moments of being decanted, the room was filled with scents of flowers, cedar and currants. It was a revealing moment on the journey.

Incidentally, *decanting* is a great way to separate *sediment* from the wine that is being served, but this is a technique unto itself. We'll explore this later.

Now, focus on the *aroma* and the *bouquet* separately and <u>*REMEMBER*</u> what you experienced. Try to remember it in terms of your *environment* at that moment. Where are you? It is amazing how *tastes* and *smells* and the *environment* can recreate a valuable point of reference!

You should now have a pretty good idea of the quality of the wine and what it may taste like. If you ever have a chance to visit *Napa Valley* in California, a "must do" is a visit to the *St. Supery Winery*. They have a wonderful educational tour that walks you through the entire production and tasting processes while offering an actual tasting.

SOUND

Simply, the *pop* of the cork or the *clink* of the glasses will satisfy this sense! That's why we clink glasses – to honor the auditory sense.

FEEL

This sensation is one of the most interesting for me. Being a musician, the experience follows the form of a sonata with its exposition, development, recapitulation and coda. I have heard literary figures draw analogies to the structure of a great novel, from the introduction right through to the denouement. Let me transpose this jargon so that we can all relate to it. First, there is the "*attack*" – that very moment when the wine actually touches our lips and the tip of the tongue. There is a very unique sensation here, for this is when we sense the *texture* and the *temperature* of the wine. The *temperature* is critically important. It can change the *character* and the *body* of the wine. Generally, the cooler the temperature, the more you will notice *acidity*. If the wine is too warm, the *acid* will fade. Thus, a *flabby* wine may appear so because it's either too warm when served or is no longer properly *balanced*. Is it *tight, diffuse* or *oily*? Is it *gritty* or *smooth*? How easily does the actual liquid make its way to other parts of the mouth? How quickly does the wine *expose* itself and make its presence known? This *touchy, feely* moment runs concurrently with the next sensation for discussion, *taste*. But let's focus on the feel for now.

This is the *exposition*, the point at which the wine starts to *reveal* itself. How does the *texture feel* on the *tongue* and *palate*, even the roof of the mouth? Does it have a *burning sensation* on the tongue? Back to the *feel* – does it feel *hot, warm* or *cold*? First of all, a *sparkling* wine will *feel* totally different from a *still* wine. In it, you can feel the *effervescence.* Some Champagnes have very, very fine, slowly rising bubbles, while others may have course, dynamic bubbles. A California *chardonnay* will feel *acidic* (like biting into a green apple) while *buttery* at the same time. This is a result of *malolactic fermentation* (*malo* from the Latin word that refers to apples and *lactic* for the softer acidity that makes it feel or even taste *buttery*). Don't forget, too, that white wines such as this need to be served chilled in order to highlight the *acidity.* In red wine, we must ask if there is any *sediment* or *gritty* substance that you can actually feel. Does it leave a *coating* on your teeth? Is it *oily?* When you finally swallow, does it *burn*, does it *go down easily*, and does it make the *cheeks want to pucker* at the back of the jaws? Does it make your *eyes water*? How does it feel seconds or moments after you have *swallowed*? Is it a *good feeling* or is it *unpleasant*? Once and most importantly, <u>*REMEMBER*</u> what it feels like as well as where you are and who you are with! Context is everything!

As an aside, when a non-wine drinker is offered a glass of fine wine, I will bet my last dollar that after grabbing the glass by the bowl and after the first sip, they will say, "Smoooooooth", as that sensation is their only point of reference.

TASTE

The time has come. You have been patient long enough and now it is time for your reward. Take some of this magical liquid into your mouth while taking in a little air at the same time. (Try not to choke or drool. This may take some practice!) *Swish* it around in your mouth but don't swallow. Each phase will reveal more and more about the wine. Now chew it. That's right, _CHEW_ it! Let it cover every inch of surface area inside your mouth. Remember that different parts of the mouth experience different things or tastes: *sweet, sour, bitter* and *salt*. Is it tart? It is the interaction of these various taste components that results in the composite taste of the wine.

While the wine is still in your mouth, you need to ask yourself some important questions. Does the wine taste anything at all like it smelled? This is the characteristic that I call *congruity*. Sometimes, a wine can smell wonderful, and taste flawed. Or a wine can smell *off* and taste wonderful. Sometimes, a wine will have no *nose* whatsoever, but *taste* like a miracle. If the wine exhibits a wonderful *nose*, but has no *taste*, this is a major disappointment. Can you taste the *fruit*? You should if it's a *young* wine – *straightforward, fruity* and *delicious*. Do you taste, perhaps, more *complex flavors* such as *oak* or *cedar*, *violets, chocolate* and *spices*, or does the taste *evolve* each second *unfolding* into layer upon layer of new discoveries? This is a sign of a wonderful and usually, mature wine, one in which the fruit has become more *subtle,* and the *tannins* softer and more complex. What it loses in *fruit* over time is made up for in *complexity, grace* and *finesse.* Did you ever bite into a *grape seed* or *stem*? I'm sure that you have, and I am also sure that you can taste it right now, just reading this. That *drying, tart* taste is *tannin.* If you taste a lot of this in a wine, it is probably very young and is worthy of some good years in your cellar before you open the next bottle from that case.

How about *body*? Is it a *big* wine, *medium* or a *light* wine? Does it *overpower* you or draw you in for a closer look? Is it a wine that you can *chew*? This characteristic is an important matter of individual taste and defines our preferences in wine. It is also useful in pairing wine with food. A big wine will *overpower* a light dish and vice versa, but more on that later. One very important observation is that a great wine is not *static*. As it is exposed to air and as it interacts with foods, the wine keeps changing, evolving, blossoming, transforming – simply getting better and better and better and the tasting experience actually becomes a wonderful conversation.

On the occasion of our twentieth anniversary, I went to my local wine supplier and was prepared to spare no expense in obtaining a fine bottle of *Champagne*, Joanne's favorite wine. I walked out of the shop with a very interesting bottle that I had never seen before. It was a textured, fluted bottle, the label said *Heidsiek Monopole Diamant Bleu*, *Brut*. I was prepared to pay over $100.00 but this bottle scanned at only $40.00. Not bad! We began our special evening. We lit a fire and decided to drink the Champagne a Capella, no food (or orchestral accompaniment in musical terms). It took us nearly two hours to finish the bottle as the wine was not conducive to drinking but begged to be sipped. The first sip was a stunner. Our eyes simultaneously met as we both experienced the very same thing. Perfect *texture*, the bubbles didn't take away any of the subtle taste or bouquet. There was ample *aroma* but the shocking thing to us was that no two sips were alike. The taste kept changing over the course of two hours – from *citrus* to *nuts*, *wheat* to *apples* and *pears*, *herbs* and *grasses* back to citrus and, keep in mind that we did not take in a bite of food the whole evening. The *aftertaste* lasted for hours - this is wine at its best and something that one never forgets. Keep in mind that wine does NOT have to be expensive.

Now the BIG question: I have often said that the most ridiculous invention was the *spit bucket* (more commonly referred to as the *pour bucket*). How can you taste such a glory of nature and then, in good conscience, spit it out?!?!?! The answer is simple.

The more wine you ingest, the *duller* your senses become. True, you will enjoy virtually ANY wine more, but we do want to be discriminating and objective. It is important that your senses remain as sharp for the fifth course wine as for the first course wine! If there are four or more wines to taste, SPIT THEM OUT!!! Just swallow a drop. Now, remember the taste just as you did the previous attributes.

FINISH

Let's examine the effect of the drop that you swallowed. How does it feel in the back of the mouth and the back of the throat? Is it *burning*? Does the taste *linger*? Is there an *aftertaste*? If so, is it a *pleasant* taste? How *long* does it linger? A minute or two later, can you still taste the wine with all of its attributes? Do you *remember* it? We have enjoyed some terrific wines that offered a finish and an aftertaste still lingering the next morning.

TASTING EXERCISE

A bottle of wine, a grape, a coffee bean,
a walnut and dark chocolate!

We can read or talk all we want, but what really matters is the actual tasting experience. I am going to offer you my favorite experiment which will get you to taste the components of the wine and internalize the experience.

Necessary items:

A full-bodied red such as a cabernet sauvignon. It does not have to be high end or expensive, just a credible wine.

A plump, juicy grape

A coffee bean

A walnut

A piece of dark chocolate

Pour the wine into the glass. Look at it, swirl it, smell it and take a sip. Chew the wine, swallow it and take in some air. Wait a minute or two. Now take the grape, eat it – chew it up well before swallowing it. Take another sip of the wine. It tastes incredibly different, doesn't it? The grape desensitized your palate to the attributes of fruit and sweetness in the wine. All you taste now are the chemical components of the wine.

Take some air into your mouth.

Next, chew the coffee beans. You have always heard of the tannins in wine. Now, sip the wine again and you can really taste them and experience the dryness, the acidity that is so characteristic of particularly young wines. The word itself has now changed from an intangible to a real tangible. Remember, the tannins are found in the skin, seeds and stems of the grapes – not very pleasant! Tannins are preservatives used in the leather industry: you have heard of tanning the leather. They enable the wine to age, not spoil and they soften over time.

So, now we must neutralize the effect of the tannins. How do we do this? Now we eat the walnut.

Walnuts are high in tannins and by chewing the walnut, it mitigates the experience of tannins in the wine and in the mouth.

Again, take in some air.

Your palate is pretty messed up by now and we need to bring it back to normal. It is time to eat the dark chocolate! Once you have chewed and swallowed it, wait about five minutes taking in air (into the mouth) and shortly, the wine will taste as it should.

SERVING WINE IN RESTAURANTS

"Lasciate ogni speranza voi ch'entrate!"

("Abandon all hope ye who enter here!")

- Dante Alighieri

Our favorite French restaurant, Le Soufflé, Paris.

Serving wine at home and ordering it in a restaurant are two very different propositions. I am combining the two here, however, because the comparisons presented are so rich and logical. There are three things that you need for a favorable wine experience. You need a *clean, clear, odor-free* wine glass. You need a functional *corkscrew*. You need a bottle of decent wine (not expensive – decent, i.e., a *wine of integrity*). Now, all of this may sound pretty basic and you're probably thinking, "I don't need this guy to tell me this obvious stuff!" But how many times have you broken a cork? How many times have you seen fingerprints or lips on your wineglass? I have news for you. They probably were not yours! POOH! YUCK! All I am trying to do at this point is develop some good habits. These three simple things are no extra expense for a restaurant either. How many times have you had to ask for a new wineglass? How many times has your server ruined a cork? How many times have you had to send back the wine and how many times did you drink wine that you should have sent back, just because you're a nice person? Point of fact, I have sent dirty wine glasses back far many more times than I have sent back the wine. This should not be. You are entitled to *clean glasses*, an *intact cork* and a *decent bottle of wine* in even the most basic restaurant. If they take on the responsibility of offering it, they must serve it properly. If you order a bottle of wine in a restaurant, it MUST be *sealed* when it arrives at your table unless other arrangements have been made previously for a very special situation. If the bottle is covered by a napkin during the uncorking and pouring, ask to see the label FIRST. You may have the right wine, but the wrong vintage and vice versa (caveat: The wrong vintage can be a costly mistake in an upscale restaurant and one that is hard to argue).

At the table, how should the wine be presented?

At home, the wine bottle should be clearly visible, and the wine should be poured into glasses/decanters that enable the wine to express itself on all levels. Never place a napkin around the bottle. This obscures the label. Try not to use colored or tinted glasses, for this obscures the clarity and alters the color of the wine. It's a typical practice on a special occasion to pull out your finest hand-cut crystal. This is all well and good and there is a time for it, but I prefer clear, unmanipulated glasses. The important thing here is that the glasses are clean and odor free.

Speaking of odor free, this sounds mean, but it also applies to the guests, that's right, the guests if expensive wines are being featured. In these cases, I inform our guests ahead of time not to wear perfumes or colognes. It can be a very uncomfortable evening for the person sitting next to a highly perfumed guest.

In what order should the wines be served?

Wines, like foods, should be served progressively. You need to progress from light to heavy. This is not my preference, necessarily, but it does flow from the natural order of things. Strong foods and wines overpower lighter foods and wines. That's just the way it is. So, courses and their accompanying wines should progress from light to heavy, light to full body with sweeter foods and wines served at the end of the meal.

Do all wines need preparation before serving?

No, not at all, but some do. What do I mean by *"prep"*? Simply, the settling of a wine with noticeable *sediment* and the acclimation to the *proper temperature*, beyond that, some *breathing* perhaps. The settling is accomplished by letting the bottle stand in the room in which it will be served for about twelve hours prior to opening. If the wine doesn't require decanting, opening the bottle in a non-molesting manner an hour or so prior to serving is all that you need. Some wines need more time than others.

At what temperature should wines be served?

Each wine has its *ideal serving temperature*. What's the ideal serving temperature? It's the one that lets the wine express itself freely and totally. It is said that red wines should be served at room temperature and that white wines need to be chilled. In a city like Buffalo, where Joanne and I make our home, room temperature covers a wide range. In summertime, it can be as high as 80° and in winter, it can be as low as 64° for those who don't like to blow their wine budget on utility bills.

When it is said that red wines should be served at room temperature, that room is likely a wine cellar, i.e., 54-64°. Most reds will really show their stuff in this range, but keep in mind that some reds should indeed be chilled. Americans tend to serve their reds too warm and their whites too cold. The difference in ideal temps range from red to white is really no more than 10° - 15° F.

Not too long ago, I had a very revealing experience. It was a beautiful late afternoon in mid-November, unusually warm, 63° F and sunny. Since our winters are so long, we try to milk every opportunity to cook outside right through the winter whenever possible. Joanne brought home a couple of Prime Delmonico steaks, so at 5:00 pm, while there was still a bit of daylight, I fired up the *'barbie'*. Here's the drill. I grab a bottle from the cellar and sip as the grill heats up. That night, I exhumed a '98 *Château Pesquie, Côtes du Ventoux* and poured a glass in the kitchen for the ritual. The wine was most pleasant indeed, *young, aromatic* (as it should be), *fruity* and *smooth as silk*, certainly not a *Pétrus*, but quite serviceable for the occasion or lack thereof. As the barbie heated up and the sun went down, the air temp reciprocated. I took another sip and much to my surprise, the wine revealed that it had some real *bones* – a *tight structure* that *balanced* and *held* together all of the attributes that I described earlier, but now the *tannins* and other *acids* started to show a bit. I kept sipping as the steaks sizzled and the wine became more *complex* and more *interesting*. I had grown to love this wine, but by the time the steaks were screaming for the plate, my glass was downright cold – I would guess 45°. All that I could taste now was *tannin* and *alcohol*. "Wow!" Had I finished this bottle at one wrong temperature, my impression of it would have been forever flawed. When the glass returned to the kitchen table, it once again started to reveal itself – remarkable, and no accident.

Though the ideal temps for each wine will vary a bit, the generalities still apply. Most *sweet whites*, including *sparkling* wines, should be served in the 45-50° range. *Champagnes* and *dry whites* in the 45-52° F range. *Quaffing wines* such as *Beaujolais* and red *country wines* would be in the next 50-55° range and fine red *Bordeaux* and red *Burgundy* at 58-64° depending upon the wine. Top-shelf white Burgundy is ideal at 55-59°.

Dalle stelle, alle stalle. La poesia è finita.

From the stars to the stalls. The poetry is finished.

Now... we all know and understand the importance of the serving temperature of the wine. Picture this. You plan a nice, high-level social evening and buy a bunch of $50.00 per bottle wines. The guests arrive, let's say six couples, and out of the mix, when the wine is served, four of the guests ask for ice cubes in the wine. What do you do? I make sure that my life insurance policies are all paid up. I am a gentleman, so I go with the flow. I will NEVER put ice into wine, nor have I ever, BUT I will give them a cup of ice ON THE SIDE, so that it can never be said that I served wine with ice cubes. An even better idea is to have a "special" wine on hand just for these "special" guests. I often refer to this "special" wine as a *"brother-in-law wine"*.

Having said that, have you ever heard of *Sangria*? A most popular and world-class delight in the proper context: My family would serve Dad's Punch for big celebrations. All you need for this is a 20-gallon galvanized steel tub used ONLY for this purpose (with the occasional exception of washing the car), five gallons of Gallo Hearty Burgundy, two cups Galliano liqueur, two cups of sugar, five sliced oranges and three sliced lemons all mixed together with a bunch of ice. THEN, top it all off with a half-gallon block of vanilla ice cream floating in the center. Come on, you know that THAT's a real party ready to happen! Aunts, uncles, cousins – young and old knew the drill. No Bordeaux here! Whenever I saw that tub in the cellar, it felt like a good time, even when washing the car.

Is cork the only material used to stop a bottle?
Not everything is sacred! Over time, almost everything changes. So has the "cork". In fact, at

many wineries around the world, it has already been replaced by a synthetic substance (not the item itself but the material), a mix of vinyl and other synthetic materials with distinct advantages over the natural material from Portuguese or Spanish cork tree bark. Environmental concerns are really a moot point here because cork is a renewable resource. Bark on cork trees grows back in about nine years and can only be harvested from trees at least twenty-five years old. In addition, each generation of bark yields a higher quality (and higher cost) of cork.

The old saying, "Wine's best friend in the glass is its worst enemy in the bottle," holds true. The nemesis, in this instance, is *air*. The sole purpose of the cork (or perhaps we should refer to it as the stopper) is to keep the wine in and the air out while being inert to the wine. In ancient times, wine was not aged, so it wasn't such a big deal. Wine was stored in ceramic or stone jars and consumed in short order. Toward the second half of the nineteenth century, when the aging of some wines was becoming accepted, the use of cork stoppers became more and more prevalent, to the point where cork became an accepted and at times, revered icon of the wine culture. But corks do have a downside. They are an organic substance that has several innate weaknesses. Corks can dry out, shrink as a result of drying out, rot and become mildewed and in short, leak from both ends. Wine can ooze out while air can leak in. BAAAAD! Some wineries are now using glass stoppers with a vinyl gasket or seal – no corkscrew needed!

Three stellar '95's — three perfect corks
(opened in 2020 with a double prong remover)

Now, the diehard purists would never accept a screw-top on a bottle of *Châteaux Margaux*, but many producers are using the new, high-tech synthetic material that looks like cork. Some even produce it in a color that looks like a wine-stained cork. These new "corks" don't rot, shrink or leak.

They even appear with the estate's logo and vintage printed on them. I personally have no problem with this and as a person with an affinity for aged wines, I will support it. There is no greater frustration for me than to open a 1995 *Châteaux Pavie Decesse* to find a bad cork and rotten wine, all in front of my special guests. Yes, this has happened and I must admit that it puts me into a most foul mood at best for the rest of the evening. But I will bet my next to last dollar that it will be eons before the new "cork" will be fully embraced by the top *crus* of Bordeaux and Burgundy.

What is the best corkscrew?

"Vous devez toujours avoir un tire-bouchon à portée de main."

"You must always have a corkscrew at hand."

- Michael Andriaccio

Simply put, any kind that gets the stopper out of the bottle with the least disturbance to the wine will suffice.

Believe it or not, there is a cult out there that is more into collecting and trading corkscrews than it is into the wine itself. That's fine, I guess – whatever lights your fire. Some people prefer collecting antique tires over antique cars. Anyway, the device has had quite a historical and technical evolution, all for the solitary task of removing the stopper from a bottle of wine. It is no endeavor to be taken lightly! A broken cork, a broken bottle or even a 'disturbed' bottle can ruin what portends to be a great culinary experience.

The mission of the corkscrew is to remove the cork with the least possible disturbance to the wine and the least amount of damage to the cork so that the wreckage doesn't turn up floating in your glass. From my perspective, the most important component of the device is not the lever or handle (or handles in the case of butterfly designs), but rather, the *worm*. That's the curly proboscis that winds its way down into the cork. Many corkscrews, particularly the cheap butterfly screws, have a single, vertical shaft with threads running its length. This is my least favorite because an inferior cork is a willing victim ready to shred upon withdrawal, like yanking a screw out of plaster. What you are left with is a corkscrew in your hands, a cork still in the bottle, and a gaping hole in the cork rendering it irremovable, not to mention the avalanche of jetsam and flotsam that could get into the wine itself.

Regardless of the lever or handle design, my worm of preference is just what it is called, a worm. It is a forged, twisted wire that literally winds its way through the cork, actually becoming a part of it. There is no straight path into, or out of the cork. Even with a more than questionable cork, it has never failed me, and I can assure you that I have removed thousands of corks. The only danger is acquiring a cheap worm that straightens itself out and leaves the cork in the bottle upon attempted extraction.

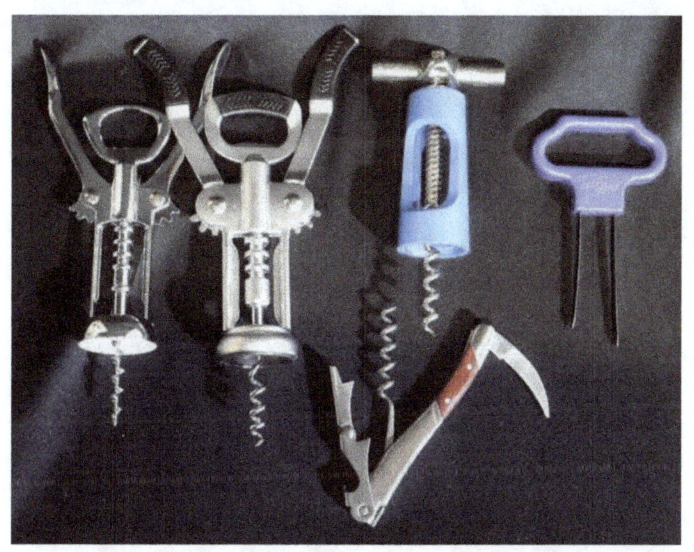

Butterfly w screw, butterfly w worm, captain's, one-way twist and double prong: the one on the far left is the least desirable.

Having discussed the worm, we are now behooved to discuss the leverage system that activates the extraction of the cork. The most popular type is the *"captain's"* or waiter's type of folding, pocketknife-like corkscrew. It is most reliable and is usually fitted with a quality worm and is easy to pocket or carry. It should NOT, however, be the only arrow in the quiver. Have you ever gone into a fine restaurant and ordered an expensive and *"aged"* wine – one

that any novice would know throws a sediment –
and then watched the server at the tableside hold
the bottle at his or her waist and shake the daylights
out of that vessel with every violent twist of the
corkscrew, then finally do a Marylou Retton double
axel as they leverage the cork out with a grand
"pop"? The next grand event should be the
immediate seizure and incarceration of the server
AND the proprietor. The wine has now been ruined
for consumption with dinner and so has the
evening. By the time the wine recovers and the
sediment settles, it's time for breakfast or at least
espresso! For these fine wines, a screw that will
accommodate cork removal from a still bottle of
wine solidly seated on the table is not only the best
option – it's the ONLY option. It can be a butterfly if
it has a real worm or the type that is placed over the
top of the bottle requiring a consistent twisting of
the device in the same direction to both penetrate
and lift the cork without disturbing the bottle. The

Captain's Screw is really quite risky with older wines in that upon extraction, the angle of the pull is such that it actually bends the cork in half – a maneuver that an aged cork may not survive.

Right

Wrong!

For very old wines with predictably problematic corks, I always use a double-prong remover (no shaft or worm). Two metal prongs, one longer than the other, are gently pushed down the sides of the cork with a back-and-forth motion. Then, a gentle twist of the handle with an upward motion will remove a fragile cork quite effectively without puncturing it.

Pour it or let it breathe?

Tutt'è bene che finisce bene!

All is well that ends well!

It depends on how badly you want to taste it. Normally, right out of the bottle is fine, that is, let it stand a couple of minutes just to let it recover from the withdrawal of the cork. Personally, since I sip my wines, I really enjoy tasting the evolution of the wine since it's been opened. Unless it's a very formal or special occasion, I'll open the bottle, then fetch the glasses. By the time I'm back to the bottle, the wine should be good to go. Most wines will react to air within the first twenty minutes to half an hour. Others, of course, take longer. You will have to glean this from experience.

Sometimes, you can really kill a wine by leaving it open too long. This is true for some very old wines. Yes, they need to breathe, but because they may be quite fragile, they offer a small window of opportunity. On one occasion, Joanne and I were invited to the home of some friends for a special dinner. We accepted on the condition that we provide the wines. BUT, I insisted that I deliver the wines the day before so that I could stand them in the dining room to acclimate for the big event. I left the hostess instructions to gently open the bottles precisely at 6:00 pm (two hours before dinner). She misunderstood. When we arrived for dinner, yes, the bottles were opened properly, but she thought that I meant at 6:00 pm the night before. These wines had been standing open for twenty-six hours! When she told me, I politely tried not to have a stroke and/or coronary on the spot. After all, she did follow the directions...to some degree. Joanne and I quietly stared at one another, knowing that the wines were going to be a disaster. WRONG! They were delicious. One was a '83 *Château Prieurée Lichine*, the other was a 1994 *Saucelito Canyon Dos Ranchos Zinfandel* and both of these wines came through in grand style. Being the gracious humanitarians that we are, our hosts don't yet know this story.

To decant or not to decant?

"To decant or not to decant, THAT is the question...whether 'tis nobler to just pour it straight into the glass or to decant it for hours", only experience will tell you.

Decanting has two objectives: the most common is simply to aerate the wine, and the other is to separate the sediment from the wine before it hits the glass. Some dear friends, Mark and Debbie, two extremely discriminating wine lovers, invited us to their favorite restaurant, the Hourglass Restaurant in Buffalo, which is no longer. The proprietor, Terry Bechakas, was famous for his 20,000+ bottle wine cellar and his uncanny knowledge of wine. In fact, his restaurant had no wine list – HE was the wine list. He wandered to each table, assessed what had been ordered for the meal and suggested the appropriate wines. We all ordered something different. Terry suggested that we begin with a '95 *St. Denis* (Burgundy). It was a beautiful wine, loyal to its *pedigree*, rose petal bouquet et al. The second wine was a '75 *Château Beychevelle* (Bordeaux). Since we were honored and gracious guests, I had no idea what the cost of the bottle was, but the wine was stunning. I had previously tasted the '76, '78, 82 & '83, but never the '75.

Tableside, Terry gingerly opened the *Beychevelle* – perfect technique – no danger at all to the cork or wine. Though it was the second wine of the night, it was opened and decanted first in order to breathe. He then brought out the St. Denis and poured it straight into the glasses. When asked about decanting or lack thereof, he explained that his good friend, the famed French wine legend, Joseph Drouhin, said that it is generally good practice to decant wines that are ten years old or more – EXCEPT FOR BURGUNDY, which he NEVER decanted. Why? Because the sediment in pinot noir-based wines is different from that of cabernet-based wines. In this case, it mostly consists of particles from the thinner grape skins, which actually serve as "filters" in the glass precipitating to the bottom and don't have the "off" taste associated with the sediment thrown from a cab. What a lesson!

Do glasses really make a difference?

A glass is a glass is a glass is a glass...NOT! I have never professed to be a Steuben Scholar or a master engineer for the Corning Glass Works, but I have sipped a great deal of wine in my day. The glass DOES make a difference. In the massive oeuvre of wine chronicles and research, volumes are readily accessible to deal with wine and a whole thesaurus of adjectives to describe it, but very little is available about the wine lover's second most valuable organ – the mouth. Arguably, the most popular information about the mouth has been created and diffused not by a physician or winemaker but rather, by *Georg Riedel*, the legendary Austrian glassmaker.

Champagne flute, Bordeaux, Burgundy, Chardonnay,
Sherry and Port.

The far-reaching Riedel enterprise is the result of passionate research into how the human mouth accepts and processes wine. Isn't this the essence of what we do? You wouldn't be reading this very book if your mouth were dysfunctional. Riedel's premise is that different areas of the mouth give us different reactions to a substance, resulting in taste. The design of the glass choreographs the way the wine enters and diffuses in the mouth. Different wines need different glasses in order to optimize the carefully orchestrated reaction of the taste buds to the introduction of a sip of wine into the mouth.

The four basic taste sensations are *sweet, sour, bitter* and *salt*, and it is the combined response to these sensations that gives us the impression of taste. No one on earth knows what another person tastes or perceives as taste. How we express it is a characterization of the essence of the beverage. Let's exaggerate for a moment. Would you drink beer from a plate? Why Not? Simply, it would be flat within a minute of the pour, thus, neutralizing one of the great and distinguishable characteristics of the beverage. That is precisely why the *Champagne flute* was created. It holds the *carbonation* permitting the bubbles to travel through more wine, focusing the aromas and expelling gas at the very rim of the glass. This is opposed to the romantic notion of the *Marie Antoinette glass* (cup-shaped, small bulbous bottom at the bowl, with a stem) fashioned after the shape of her esteemed breast. Though, I take great pleasure in the thought of drinking from a cup in the very shape of that storied and venerated gland, let us remember that it was uniquely designed for the dispensation of one nectar only, not Champagne. I would prefer to hold that thought while I sip fine Champagne from a properly suited flute for a TOTAL experience, if you get my drift!

It gets even more specific than that. The lips and tongue are the first point of contact for the taste buds. As stated earlier, the initial impressions we get from a sip are *temperature* and degree of *sweetness*. These sensors are located at the tip of the tongue. The sour sensors or buds are found on the sides of the tongue and the salty ones after the sour. The bitter buds are way in the back. So, you can see how the glass can make all of the difference in the world. Though *Riedel* produces a specific glass for virtually every type of wine, this doesn't mean that you need a warehouse full of glasses to enjoy wine. Three glasses can work well in any home but if you do get the opportunity to try the other glasses with their respective wines, it will blow you away. The most important concern about the wineglass is that it has a *stem*, and is sparkling clean, clear and odor free.

How much wine should be poured into the glass?

A wineglass should be filled only to the widest part of the bowl. This enables maximum surface area to concentrate the esters up the chimney of the glass to be focused at the rim. Generally, only about four ounces of wine should be present in the glass. A 750ml bottle will offer 5+ servings.

Does it really matter how the glass is held?

Surely, you have seen pictures of supposedly knowledgeable people holding their wine glasses by the stems or even by the base of the glass. Many people see this and think, "Ooooh, hoity, toity. Look at those snobs!" Well, those snobs are really doing it right. For whatever reason they're doing it, the technique is important. One of the beauties of the sensual wine experience is the sight – the look of the wine in the glass. A cloudy, fingerprinted glass is very unappealing and doesn't give you the opportunity to see the clarity and color of the wine. Also, your hand on the bowl of the glass changes the temperature of the wine and, therefore, affects the taste. In addition, holding the glass by the stem or the base enables you to freely swirl the wine in the glass before sniffing it. When you hold the glass by the bowl, you also run the risk of picking up food or other odors from the fingers – odors that will alter or bury the scent of the wine. This is particularly important with Champagne.

Right.

Wrong.

How should the glassware be washed?

Foreign elements introduced into a glass of wine, particularly fine wine, can be disastrous. Not only is it important that a clean glass be dry before the introduction of wine, but it is also imperative that it be free of soap or detergent. Have you ever been presented with a sparkling glass, then, when the wine is poured in, multicolored bubbles appear from nowhere – lots of bubbles, each with its own spectrum of color? Where's Lawrence Welk when you need him? It's very difficult to thoroughly rinse a glass that has had soap or detergent poured directly into it. It is also important that the glass be clean and free of germs. I have found that if dish soap is poured directly into the glass and then the glass is washed, the soap will cling tenaciously to the glass and rinse after rinse will not remove it. If hot, soapy water is put into an already wet glass, it is more readily removed with a single rinse. Using very hot water is important. The same applies to decanters which are even more difficult to rinse because of the small openings. I am often asked by folks who don't know me, "What do you do in your spare time?" My response, "I wash glasses."

Let's go back to the restaurant. To me, it only makes sense to serve any food in a manner that enhances the food or at least the experience. I don't mean that you have to go through an elaborate ceremony each time you serve a glass of wine, but I do think that just a little care should go into the process or simply, one should develop some good habits. Like anything else, when you do it enough, it becomes a habit. It really bothers me when I go into a restaurant, let's say, an Italian restaurant, where the server mispronounces all of the names of the dishes, brushetta for *bruschetta* (brus-kay'-tta), pennay for *penne* (payn'-nay), or the ever-popular redundancies like *fettuccini* noodles. Hello! Fettuccini ARE noodles. "Oh yes, I would like some noodles noodles." When you go out and pay for something, you would expect to have it delivered to you by professionals who know something about what they are doing.

Without any extra expense and only a bit more effort, most restaurants could drastically improve their tableside handling of wine. Did you ever notice that when you are first seated at a table in a restaurant, there is already a wine glass at the setting? Why is it that when you order wine from the wine list, that they remove that clunky old thing and replace it with a real wine glass? Shouldn't the real wine glass have been there at the onset?

Joanne's bruschetta.

Whenever you go out for a dining experience, it only makes sense that a special wine would cap off the event. Wine in restaurants, however, is very tricky business and unless you have an unlimited budget, it is probably best for most people to be very conservative and not expect too much from the wine side of the evening. There are far too many variables and constraints. First of all, to get a really good bottle, it will cost as much as four entrees. Secondly, chances are that not everyone in the party will appreciate it. Third, unless all guests order the same appetizers and entrées, the wine may not be appropriate. Fourth, for me, it really hurts to see a bottle selling for $100 when I know I have a case at home for which I paid $30.00 a bottle. Fifth, the restaurant may have a respectable wine list, but the help may know nothing about the wines. Case in point: Joanne and I were at a finer establishment, a Tuscan restaurant with a great wine list and extraordinary specials. I had ordered a *Battasiolo Barbaresco* to start. The restaurant was dark and when the young server approached me with the bottle to show me the label, I immediately recognized the *Battasiolo* label and nodded positively to go ahead and open it. As she left the table, I realized that I hadn't seen the entire label, so I summed her back. She once again showed me the bottle and as I suspected, it was the *Battasiolo Barolo*, not the *Barbaresco*. She still didn't realize that there was a difference. Finally, we were served the *Barbaresco*, but on our way home, we checked our receipt and discovered that we were charged for the *Barolo* – an overcharge of $20.00. Watch out and don't trust even the most ostensibly experienced server. CHECK THE LABEL AND BEFORE YOU LEAVE, CHECK THE BILL! AND IF THE WINE IS NOT UP TO EXPECTATIONS, DON'T HESITATE TO SEND IT BACK! The proprietor did not pay nearly as much for it as you will have. On one occasion, six of us were in a high-end steakhouse, and only one of us was a nonalcohol drinker. Much to my amazement, he sent back his Pepsi! So don't be bashful about sending back defective or incorrect wine. If you have to really think about whether or not it is good, it isn't.

There is nothing at all wrong with ordering wines by the glass. Each diner can be accommodated, and if it is a respectable place, it will offer a fine variety of wines by the glass. We all know that the wine glass should only be filled to the widest point of the bowl, however, if you are ordering by the glass, you should expect to be served a FULL serving. If a bottle is ordered, servers like to fill the glasses so that another bottle will have to be ordered soon thereafter. Don't let this happen when you order a bottle. Tell them to fill the glasses only halfway at most.

Another problem with ordering fine wines in restaurants is the advance prep of *older* or *heavier* wines that need *decanting*. You can call ahead, but you will be charged for the wine if you cancel your reservation.

Tableside serving of restaurant wines reveals a great deal about the server and the establishment. See my section on uncorking wine. I will never forget a wonderful dinner experience I shared with Joanne, my sister, my two sisters-in-law and my niece in Montepulciano, Tuscany at the *Caffè Poliziano*, home of the famous *Vino Nobile di Montepulciano* of the same name. We were situated on the outdoor terrace overlooking the cypress-studded vineyards of Tuscany just before sunset. The server approached the table with a bottle of their '93 Vino Nobile Riserva and six sparkling, large bowl glasses. Typically, the nose of Vino Nobile is quite timid and needs a bit of coaxing to reveal itself. She proceeded to pour about an inch of wine into one glass, then rigorously swirled the wine so that it coated every millimeter of the inside of the glass.

She then poured that very same bit of wine from that glass into another glass and repeated the ritual. She used those same drops of wine over and over with all of the glasses in order to *"season"* them and prepare them to receive and caress their elegant guest, the wine. It is a strikingly vivid memory of both the ritual and the sensory overload from that special occasion and bottle of wine. It was also evident that we had a sophisticated server. As an aside, this is typical in European restaurants as a waiter or server position is a career or profession, not just a temporary, part-time job.

As I said before, wine can be enjoyed at any level, so let's start with the basics. At the end of a long workday (every day in our home) Joanne and I unwind and catch up on each other's experiences of the day with a ritual. I go down into the cellar, grab a bottle of wine, bring it up, grab two REAL wine glasses, open up the bottle, pour the wine right into the glasses (only up to the widest point of the glass, of course) and that's it. We sip and talk and every single night – it is special. Sometimes, we'll plan an EXTRA special night by targeting a specific bottle of wine ahead of time. If it's an older wine, I'll bring it up the day before and let it stand in the room, and if possible, I'll open it an hour before we pour it. Then, there are other formal, special occasions, that require a careful selection of wine and food, the proper prep and decanting, if necessary, along with the appropriate glasses for the wine, etc.

The point is, the more special you make the presentation, the more the wine and the experience will reward you. A great wine in a goblet is still a great wine. It just won't speak to you with all that it has to say. An everyday cabernet, however, in a *Riedel Cabernet* glass will seem like a much greater wine than it really is. That's because the glass enables the wine to express itself without inhibition or outside influence. You will detect things in this ordinary wine that went right past your lips in that clunky old glass that I referred to earlier.

I'm sure that on various occasions, you have opened a bottle of your favorite wine. Usually, the taste is just what you would expect, but sometimes, the wine tastes great and other times, it is lacking in something nondescript or intangible. Can it be that the same wine can vary from bottle to bottle? Yes, but this is not likely. What is happening is that the elements surrounding and influencing the wine and the drinker are variable and in flux. Every wine has an *optimum serving temperature*, an *optimum interval for breathing*, requires a clean palate and a proper or consistently shaped *glass*. As in tennis or golf, there is a sweet spot. In the case of red wines, *cooler* temperatures tend to inhibit the *flavors,* while *warmer* temps tend to *neutralize* the *acid* and make them seem *flabby*. You may have eaten something with a *lingering aftertaste* that is neutralizing elements of the wine, or the food accompanying the wine is changing the way in which you perceive it. Like a fine painting, the subject must be *properly framed*.

As an appropriate aside, you would expect a winery tasting room to be a shrine that reverently presents its relics in such a way as to evoke adoration and respect. The sip should transcend all memories of the day at hand. You can tell a great deal about a wine operation just by stepping into the tasting room. I recently took a drive through *New York's Finger Lakes* wine region – an absolutely lovely part of the world with far more potential than even the locals can imagine. Many small wineries here are competing for attention and recognition of the quality wine that they can produce. As evident as the battle for market share is, I was astounded that in three consecutive tastings at different and neighboring wineries, each one a recognizable name in wine shops, how little was done to enhance the wine or at least, let it freely express all that it had to offer. In some cases, the staff actually unwittingly sabotaged the cause. Now, the things that I'm pointing out are not money-intensive procedures, in fact, the improvements that I'm suggesting don't cost an extra cent. First of all, at one estate, the glasses were cloudy and even dirty. This shows that they are only <u>rinsed</u> after tastings and not washed. If this lack of attention is inherent in the serving of the wine, I can't help but think that it goes deeper into the production of the wine. One glass even had lipstick on it – totally reprehensible! When I'm tasting wine, I don't want to be kissing some invisible stranger by proxy.

Another faux pas was the presence of Keebler saltine crackers on the bar to supposedly *"cleanse the palate"* between wines. Are they kidding or what?! *Salt* destroys all *fruit* in the wine and *enhances* the *alcohol.* It's a totally different wine after the cracker. Then, each glass was rinsed out between wines, not dried, just rinsed. Now, I do understand that it isn't feasible to always have a dishwasher person on hand, but the introduction of water, especially sizable quantities of water, into a wine totally changes its *structure* and *chemical balance*, particularly if the wines are already *loosely structured* or *lightweights.* In one case, a customer asked to taste the jam and grape juice produced by the property, then asked to taste the wine. Shouldn't the staffer have advised this person that if they were planning to taste wine, they should do it before tasting the jam and juice? Then these proprietors wonder why they are not considered to be on the cutting edge of the world wine scene. Is it bias or persecution? I think neither. It is dilettantism and I assure you that there is no fine line between that, and art. Make no mistake, these are talented, well-meaning, committed and hard-working individuals who need a little bit of exposure and guidance so that they can compete on the world market. There is so much potential, and they are, oh so close. These proprietors ought to charter a plane and head to *Napa Valley* for a weekend to see how it should be done or, better yet, go to Europe, where the experience of thousands of years is obvious in the product of even the smallest producers. The Europeans know the difference between craft and art. It is a state of mind. European winemakers believe that they are artists, while many American vintners take pride in being craftsmen. I have seen countless paintings, tapestries, and sculptures in European enotecas, but there, I have never seen a powder blue wooden duck sporting a calico hat. Too many American tasting rooms are full of them.

PART 3

SEDIMENTAL JOURNEYS CONTINUED

CELLARING AND STORING WINE

A wonderful trio from the great 1995 vintage.

There are a lot of reasons why someone would want to have a wine cellar. Some just get off on saying that they have one. I have met individuals who have cellars of several thousand bottles. When asked what they have, they stammer & stutter because they don't really know or care. They can simply afford to buy a lot of high-priced wine. Others store wines for potential investment reward, and others, like me, want to acquire young, *age-worthy* wines while they are still cheap and hold them until they blossom into maturity. After fifty years now, if I want a $600.00 bottle of wine for dinner, all I have to do is go downstairs and grab a bottle that I bought twelve years ago for about $35.00. I'm not in it for the monetary return on investment. I do it because I love great wine. But, whatever the reason, in order to build a cellar over time, you must be disciplined.

In addition to selecting the right wines for your cellar, you either have to buy more that you can drink now, or drink less now so that you have some for later. There is one criterion that you should have a handle on before you start buying wines for future consumption, *proper storage conditions*. Wine is a living thing – it is constantly evolving, but in order for it to evolve favorably, proper storage conditions MUST exist. All you really need is a dark, cool, not-too-dry place and vibration-free where the bottles can lay down undisturbed until harvest time. Though cool temperatures are important, it is more important that temperature changes are not frequent, are not sudden and not radical or extreme. You can get away with a slightly warmer temperature than the ideal if the temperature remains somewhat constant. Higher temperatures cause the wine to mature more rapidly. You certainly don't want the wine to freeze, get too hot or be exposed to any kind of direct or bright light, particularly sunlight.

RULE #1: HAVE A PROPER PLACE TO STORE YOUR WINE.

People ask me time and time again, "What wines should I stock in my cellar?" The answer is simple and is...

RULE #2: STOCK THE WINES YOU LIKE TO DRINK.

If it's your cellar, you are the only one that you have to please. You don't even have to impress anyone, so if you have 1000 bottles of $7.00 per bottle of wine and it is wine you like and it will keep, your cellar is perfect for you. But let's talk about one of the great advantages of having a cellar. Selection!

Ninety percent of the time, the wine you drink is accompanied by food and not every wine is well suited to every type of food, so you want to have some variety and versatility in your stock.

RULE #3: VARIETY.

Even if you have a very strong preference for a particular style of wine, there are plenty of wines in that very style that are light, medium, or full-bodied. Right there, you have the basis for some diversity. If you couple that with reds and whites of the same region or style, the diversity and collection become more eclectic.

Value and milking the discount: Most wine purveyors will offer discounts of 10, 15 or even 20% on a case purchase of wine usually, even on mixed cases. Of course, you will want to benefit from a discount on expensive wines for your cellar, but a case of great wine can be as much as a mortgage payment. You don't want to do this regularly if you don't have to and guess what? You don't have to. In order to take advantage of this, buy mixed cases with one or two expensive bottles and ten or eleven everyday wines. In this way, you will be buying great wines at a discount and buying them in the same proportion that you will be consuming them.

Let's talk a bit about ageing. The WINES, that is. We touched on it earlier, but we must remember that not all wines are suitable for ageing. In fact, MOST wines are not. Sure, most red wines will benefit from a year or two in the bottle, but I'm talking about five, ten and even twenty years out. For these wines, you need to do a little homework on the types of grapes and wines that are predisposed to laying down, along with gathering some info on the way the wine was made. This, with some knowledge of the vintage and harvest conditions, should give you all that you need to know for choosing wines that you wish to lay down. The best way is to buy a case of your favorite wine and try a bottle every year or two. As the wine becomes more approachable, you speed up your consumption. If it is still hard as nails, make a note that it needs to be tasted a couple more years down the road. If it's starting to go downhill, throw a party.

RULE #4: DO YOUR HOMEWORK.

Here are some general hints. As you now know, the cabernet sauvignon grape is probably the variety that is most predisposed to ageing. You may recall that the reason for this is that the size of its pip or seed is proportionally larger relative to the mass of the grape berry, and it is the seed, along with the skins and stems, that contains the most tannin. Also, any wine that carries a *"riserva"* or "reserve" designation is a wine that has spent a good deal of time ageing in barriques or other types of oak casks. The oak adds tannin to the wine and generally, these oak-aged wines will lay down quite well and in fact, could benefit from a good deal of additional bottle age. Many wines are slow to mature, even in perfect conditions. The fine *Grand Crus* of Bordeaux require twenty to thirty years to really sing. These are the exceptions, however. Except for my everyday wines, most of the wines in our cellar will be consumed seven to fifteen years from vintage.

RULE #5: LESSER IN GREAT AND GREAT IN LESSER.

Assuming that you are like me and on a limited budget, here is a good rule of thumb when buying *Grands Crus*. It is no secret that they are prohibitively expensive, particularly in great vintages. You may want to consider purchasing the second label of these great *crus* in the finest vintages or even a second - fifth growth. The grapes are of such quality in these years that the 'lesser' châteaux produce dynamite wines in the same style for a fraction of the price. In not-so-great years, demand is lower and grape selection is more severe so that the first growths are more affordable and still produce marvelous wines typical of their pedigree, while the lesser estates will put out ordinary wines at best. Again, this is a broad concept but one that has served me well over the past fifty years.

RULE #6: SET REALISTIC TIME FRAMES.

Wine is a lifelong journey and as with any such journey, many opportunities present themselves along the way. There are "life-changing" events that confront all of us and a special occasion can become even more special if you take advantage of the fact that you have something quite precious – a wine cellar. Let me give you an example.

In 1989, I brought my young niece, Audrey, and nephew, Chris, down into the cellar and I guided them to a couple of special bins. I said, "Hey guys, want to have some fun? Pick out a bottle each. What I'll do is tag the bottle, hold it for you and we'll pull it out when you're older for a very special occasion." They touched two bottles in the same bin. Well, it must be in the blood because they picked out two bottles of a very special wine, *1983 Château Gruaud-Larose, St. Julien*, a great *deuxieme cru* or second growth from *Bordeaux*. When Chris was married in 1996, guess what wine was served at the head table. You guessed it. When Audrey was married in 2000, guess what wine she had at the head table. That's right! I paid $18.00 a bottle for them and at the time of Audrey's wedding, that bottle was going for over $300.00 on the auction market. Well, Chris works fast. He had been married five years and had four gorgeous children. Guess what I did. Yep! I went out and bought a case of 1995 Château Gruaud-Larose and tagged a bottle for each one of his four kids and that wine will probably be right at its peak when these kids are in their twenties. The remaining bottles will be tagged for other "special" family occasions (or...Joanne and I might just decide to drink them!). This particular wine is now a family "heirloom" wine. Everyone in the family, wine afficionado or not, recognizes the name of this wine and the significance that it has in our lives. Speaking of special occasions, I just know that when I die, there is going to be a party at our house following the funeral. I can see it now ... there'll be a mad dash for the cellar, great bottles will be uncorked and consumed en mass and the refrain, "He would have wanted it this way!" will be resounding throughout the neighborhood! So,

RULE #7: MAKE THE MOST OF THE "SPECIAL" NATURE OF YOUR WINE CELLAR.

Rewind!

RULE #1. HAVE A PROPER PLACE TO STORE YOUR WINE.

RULE #2. STOCK THE WINES YOU LIKE TO DRINK.

RULE #3. VARIETY.

RULE #4. DO YOUR HOMEWORK.

RULE #5. SET YOUR BUDGET AND STICK TO IT.

RULE #6. SET REALISTIC TIME FRAMES.

RULE #7. MAKE THE MOST OF THE "SPECIAL" NATURE OF YOUR CELLAR.

NATURE'S GIFTS – OIL AND BALSAMIC

Olive Oil

The Fruits of One's Labor

As a result of being classical musicians our entire lives, we've been drawn to other aspects of life that require the same passion, patience, discipline and attention to detail. With all of this said, the final product is a performance over which one doesn't always have total control due to various extraneous elements in the concert hall. We liken the art of making olive oil and wine to all other creative disciplines in which these qualities are requisite, but in olive oil and wine, the control of the final product often rests in the hands of Mother Nature. For centuries, the legendary olive tree, like the grapevine, has lured great artists the likes of Garcia Lorca, van Gogh (eighteen magnificent depictions on canvas), Cézanne, Renoir, Aldous Huxley and many others. These luminaries immortalized the olive tree on canvas, in their books and in their poems! Since Etruscan times, the olive branch has been a universally accepted symbol of peace and the wood of the tree itself has been a much sought-after species for artisans of all types.

The process of making a great olive oil is not commonly known, so let's examine it from a distance to get a better handle on how it comes to anoint our tables.

In stunningly gorgeous areas of the world such as the Mediterranean, the Middle East and America's West Coast among others, olive trees thrive. These exotic areas provide the perfect backdrop for olive trees as they worship abundant sunshine, mild winters, sufficient rain in autumn and spring and hot, dry summers with Mediterranean-type breezes. A hearty and quick-growing plant, the olive tree undergoes a period of winter dormancy from November through February, with the growing cycle reoccurring in March. The prized fruit makes its appearance in May and June, soaking up as much sun as it can get until it ripens in October. The critical and arduous task of harvesting then takes place from October through December; however, due to microclimatic differences, the schedule will vary in some locations. As in the vineyard, there is a tremendous amount of pressure on the producer to determine the absolutely right moment for harvesting the fruit so that the olives are at their ripest. Waiting even a day to begin the harvest risks the onset of rain that will dilute the juice upon pressing both grapes and olives. To further complicate things, pressing _must_ take place 24 to 48 hours after the harvest in order to achieve an olive oil of distinction. Bruised or cracked olives are discarded because they will lessen the quality of the oil by increasing the acidity level. They are also very susceptible to bacteria and rot.

The HARVEST is as personal to the producer as an instrument or brush is to the artist. As in other disciplines, there are several methods implemented for the process. The most expensive is handpicking. It is the most traditional and ensures the highest quality because it allows for on-site selection of only the highest quality fruit. Poling is a technique that requires whipping of the treetops to encourage the olives to drop into nets so that they don't hit the ground and split. The last method is machine harvesting which involves the mechanical shaking of the trees. Once harvested and selected, the olives are then WASHED, leaves are removed but the pits are retained because they, like grape seeds, contain valuable preservatives.

Now, we move to the CRUSHING stage in which the above material is reduced into a mash referred to as *"pasta"* which is then spread onto mats stacked one on top of the other in pancake fashion, then pressed to release the liquid from the "pasta". The extract from the pasta is a mix of oil, water and suspended solids that if left in the mix would taint the oil. So a process of SEPARATION by means of a centrifuge is employed to separate the water from the oil. The oil is then left for approximately one month to DECANT, allowing the remaining particles to drop to the bottom. The final "optimal" stage is FILTERING. Filtering removes all the suspended particles and leaves a clear oil. It must be noted, however, that the question to filter or not to filter is predicated upon the producer's preference and is a continual topic of passionate debate. Many argue that unfiltered oils are better in taste and yield greater health benefits. You be the judge!

All these critical stages must be completed in a timely, well-coordinated manner under the cleanest of conditions and with the guidance of a well-trained eye that knows exactly when to pick – even when Mother Nature decides not to work in conjunction with the calendar! As you can now see, patience, timing, great attention to detail and above all, passion for the art of olive production will yield an exceptional product. (And of course... Mother Nature) Enjoy your tasting!

What to look for when buying Olive Oil.

Joanne and I use olive oil in all of our meals and meal prep. We seldom use butter. You want to be sure to use quality oil, always extra virgin, but it shouldn't be expensive. Olive oil breaks down with heat, so you don't want to use an expensive oil for cooking. Once the food is prepared and platted, use a high-quality extra virgin oil as a condiment.

As with wine, the label will tell you a great deal about what's inside the bottle. Unlike wine, olive oil does not age well at all – the younger and fresher, the better.

There is Virgin Olive Oil and Extra Virgin Olive Oil. The name is determined and controlled by the *Consorzio* or Council; the highest and best grade is, of course, Extra Virgin Olive Oil. There are supermarket-level brands and Single Estate brands which are the highest quality and have the greatest health benefits. Supermarket brands are useful for cooking, and they contain monounsaturated fats. The single estate Extra Virgin Oils have more polyphenols and low acidity, .8% or less (really high-quality oils are less than .5% and usually between .15 and .3%), whereas the others have much higher acidity levels up to over 2.0%. Even supermarket brands of Extra Virgin Olive Oil are now placing this information on the label. The Single Estate Oils do not require transportation of the olives as they are crushed on-site immediately after harvest, therefore, they are fresher and contain more of the healthy attributes than the other oils, which are often blends of olives or oils from many countries. The lesser brands are also mechanically manipulated to keep the acidity levels down.

Hi-end Extra Virgin Olive Oil as a condiment.

As I mentioned before, always use extra virgin olive oil, lesser brands for cooking and use the highest quality as a condiment after plating the food.

BALSAMIC

Family Values, Medieval Style:

One thousand gallons of Balsamic in the attic.

Treasures in the attic of Acetaio di Giorgio, Modena

In our pursuit of the origins of exquisite Italian culinary traditions, we recently visited the medieval city of Modena to trace the roots of cherished balsamic vinegar. The experience was a revelation far beyond our expectations. Perhaps you are as puzzled as we have been by this curious condiment that raises some very simple and common questions. Why such a high price for vinegar? Why can I purchase a 750ml bottle for $12.00 and then see a 3 oz. bottle selling for $150.00 or more? What makes this condiment different from others? How is it made? Vinegar is vinegar, right?

Our balsamic fantasy began upon arrival in the beautiful city of Modena. Though the city has the requisite *Duomo* (Cathedral) situated on the mandatory *Piazza*, there is a strange, underlying reverence that is pervasive here in this neighbor to Bologna – the culinary capital of Emilia Romagna. Everywhere you turn, there is art and history, but here, the tradition includes the centuries-old production of balsamic vinegar.

After visiting numerous vineyards and olive groves in the miraculous Tuscan countryside, we expected the same ambiance when visiting the vinegar producers or *acetaie* (pronounced *ah-chay-tie'-ay*). This was our first surprise. Having made an appointment to visit the Acetaio di Giorgio, a small, artisanal producer, we expected another bucolic day in the country, but instead, we were dropped off at the private home of Giorgio Barbieri and Giovanna Cati right in the heart of town. After a brief introduction and exchange of formalities, they escorted us into their relatively new home (only about two hundred years old) and up one flight of stairs, then another and yet another. As we ascended the ancient escalade, we noticed that the air was taking on a subtle character that intensified as we ascended higher and higher until finally reaching the attic. From behind a closed door, a seductive and intense yet complex aroma beckoned us. As Giovanna opened the door, we were greeted by row upon row of ancient wooden barrels of various sizes filled with high-end balsamic vinegar in the making. They were meticulously lined up like ancient sentinels. As Giovanna's momentum grew and her passion for the topic became contagious, she narrated the whole story.

Much to our discovery, most production of authentic balsamic vinegar is a cottage industry, i.e., it is produced in private homes and the tradition goes back well over five hundred years. In the fifteen hundreds, the noble Estense and Ferrara families harvested a bumper crop of *trebbiano* grapes, the same used in the exquisite Tuscan dessert wine, *Vin Santo*. The quality was so high that they tried to store the excess must or juice in whatever barrels they could find, but lacking enough cellar space, they had to store them in the attic. These were trying times, and due to war after war, the barrels and their contents were forgotten for as long as 30 years. When the barrels were ultimately retrieved, the odors and tastes were so incredible that all the noble families wanted to share in the riches, and none was to be outdone. It was discovered that the ageing of the must in the uninsulated attic was just the right circumstance for it to convert to vinegar, due to the extreme seasonal temperature changes. The heat of the summer would further the process of maceration while the cold of winter provided the requisite rest, and the cycle would continue for at least ten years in order to develop great complexity and depth. This vinegar is not made from wine, but directly from the must or juice of the pressed grapes BEFORE it ever ferments – there is no fermentation. In fact, there is still debate as to whether it should be referred to as "vinegar" (derivation of the word – *vin aigre*, French for sour wine).

The production of balsamic vinegar then became a status symbol. Each family produced its own and imbued it with a personal style and character. Keep in mind that up until only sixty years ago, balsamic vinegar was never sold commercially. It was only available for a price at pharmacies for medicinal purposes as a digestive or throat potion, among other similar uses. It was a family asset used as a dowry for daughters or as payment for the best medical treatment, legal advocacy or even to pay homage to someone in an exalted social position. Whenever a daughter was born, a new batch or cycle of balsamic vinegar was begun for the family of the groom-to-be.

Let's examine a bit of the actual process of making authentic, *Traditional Balsamic Vinegar* – the one that commands the highest price. The Italian word for vinegar is *aceto* (pronounced *ah-chay'-toh*) and the authentic substance we're discussing here is *Aceto Balsamico Tradizionale di Modena*. It all begins with the *must* of the grapes being simmered over an open flame to reduce it by as much as 70% before undergoing a slow and complicated ageing process. It is then placed into a *"mother barrel"*, a 60-liter oak vat. The process involves the slow and calculated transfer of the juice from larger barrels to smaller ones and is known as *"topping off"*. When the content of the smaller barrel reduces by about a third due to evaporation and oxidation, it is topped off with juice from the next larger barrel in the cycle and so forth all the way back up the line. The content from the 60-liter barrel (the youngest juice) then tops off the 50-liter barrel of chestnut, then to a 40-liter barrel of ash, followed by a 30-liter of cherry to a 20 liter of mulberry (the oldest juice) with the cycle repeating. The smaller the barrel, the older the vinegar and the more concentrated and syrupier the content will be. The woods and cycle of woods chosen vary from producer to producer in order to create an individual and distinct style. It is the oxidation of the juice that transforms it into vinegar without fermentation.

We've learned that olive oil and wine are highly regulated products. Aceto Balsamico Tradizionale di Modena is no different. This legal designation is bestowed only by the *Corsorzio Tra Produttori dell'Aceto Balsamico Tradizionale di Modena*, the governing body. The criteria are stringent. There can be no preservatives and the product is judged by its color, smell, and taste – balance of sweet and bitter and the acidity level of 6 – 6.5%. The Consortium retains numbered samples for five years for reference or to settle any disputes over authenticity. But it doesn't end here. Even the packaging is controlled for regional identity and integrity. It can only be sold in 100 ml, bulb-shaped bottles with rectangular bases, each with a numbered seal. A white label must represent a product at least twelve years old and the gold label is reserved for the Extra Vecchio or Extra Old balsamic vinegar of at least twenty-five years. Though you can purchase balsamic vinegars of forty or even fifty years and older, the Consorzio can only certify an age of up to twenty-five years.

The city of Reggio Emilia is also a balsamic-producing locale with its own Consorzio, strict regs and slightly differing label requirements.

Perhaps now you can understand why this product is so specialized and yet, so varied. A bit later, we'll examine the three categories of Balsamic and their recommended uses. As an aside, the Italian American slang term for heartburn is the same word for vinegar or acid, *aceto*, but in this dialect, the accent falls on the first syllable (*ah'-chay-toh*). "Hey, you're giving me Aceto!"

Now, we'll explore it from the perspective of the consumer since it can cost over $150.00 for a 3-ounce bottle!

It is important to understand that this is not "wine" vinegar or vinegar made from wine, but rather a vinegar made from the must or juice of the grapes BEFORE it ever ferments and becomes wine. The juice is "cooked down" and then passed from larger barrel to smaller, barrel to barrel over decades as it evaporates – each barrel consisting of a different species of hardwood. It takes about eight hundred gallons of juice to make thirty gallons of vinegar (and that's before the barrel process!). Factor in the years of storage and you can appreciate the cost of production, hence, that of the product. The Aceto

Balsamico Tradizionale di Modena and that of Reggio Emilia are each governed by a Consorzio that guarantees authenticity, origin and quality.

When doling out high prices for this vinegar, the consumer must be aware that there are three "styles" or "grades" of balsamic vinegar. These are Artisan, Industrial and Imitation. Unless you know a little bit about what signs to look for, it's easy to be misled, for outside of the two "classified" production areas of Modena and Reggio Emilia, there is no governing body or control.

The official classification of Balsamic Vinegar began with the Duchy of Este. Records dating back to 1556 in the Este Ducal Archive indicate that they were very serious about the quality standards of this fluid, which, until the 1980s, rarely made it out of the area of production. It was almost always produced by private family concerns until the post-World War II era, when commercial production became more prevalent. In the 1970s, when culinary attitudes started to globalize, Italian chefs realized that the extremely intense flavors were conducive to the "new" international cuisine. The better the vinegar, the more balanced and harmonious the elements of sweetness and acidity, not to mention the complexity. As we travel through the styles from top to bottom, this balance dissipates and the substance loses focus, just as going from single estate wines and olive oils to the more commercially proliferated brands do.

As foreigners were introduced to Balsamic Vinegar in Modena and Reggio Emilia, demand grew and so did the number of imitators. In the late '70s, 1.75 million liters of imitation balsamic vinegar were produced vs. only 1,760 liters of the real thing, Aceto Balsamico Tradizionale di Modena (or Reggio Emilia). That is staggering, especially when you consider that the imitations will often be sold for the same price!

The imminent range war between Modena and Reggio Emilia over the right to claim authenticity was resolved in 1987 with a government decree creating a *Dual Domain of Control*. The product from Reggio Emilia is generally a bit sweeter and plummier than that of Modena. Aceto Balsamico Tradizionale can ONLY hail from Modena and Reggio Emilia. The operative word here is *Tradizionale*. If it's from anywhere else, it's not the real thing. There are, however, some tasty concoctions prepared by a young generation of Artisan-style producers striving for quality and hybrid techniques, but they just don't concern themselves about blessings from the Consorzio. These products cannot use the word *Tradizionale*. Let us now examine each classification.

"Artisan" is authentic, and its history of production goes back one thousand years. Every bottle of Aceto Balsamico Tradizionale is numbered, tested and approved by the Consorzio and averages 20 – 30 years of age. In both towns, the capsules of the bottles are color-coded, i.e., in Modena, white indicates younger, gold means Extra Vecchio. In Reggio Emilia, the bottle carries a red seal, with the indications on the red label of *Tradizionale* (around $130 for 100 ml), silver label *Qualitá Superiore* ($150) and the gold labeled Extra Vecchio ($175) in ascending order of Quality. It is very thick, coating the sides of the bottle when tipped, reminiscent of port, plums, chocolate and vanilla from all the contact with various woods.

The *"Industrial"* product is as it sounds, and it does serve nicely in the proper context on salads or when mixed into a dressing. This is more acidic than sweet and is made without the effects of time and the quality and taste vary markedly. It can be found in fancy bottles and can cost as much as the real thing because the assumption is that no one would ever know. Many additives such as wine, wine vinegar, sugar, caramel, even wood chips go into the barrel before bottling. Most often, it is a mixture of other components not permitted in the Tradizionale. Some of the better producers of this Industrial version are Giusti (we had the opportunity to personally tour the facility in Modena), Manicardi and Fini. Look for the designations API MO or API RE depending upon origin in Modena or Reggio Emilia. If you're buying from a good source, the price can be an indication of quality, but not always.

As you might suspect, the *Imitation grade* is not produced by authentic methods but is usually labeled Aceto Balsamico di Modena and this accounts for about 2/3rds of the market. Imitation vinegar is made in one day because the time-intensive processes of fermentation and oxidation are nonexistent. Colorings and flavors are added to impart some depth and the appearance of age, but the Tradizionale gets its color from the actual caramelized grape must and extract from years of contact with wood. Again, notice the absence of the word Tradizionale.

As far as uses for high-quality Balsamic Vinegar go, the possibilities are endless. The *Extra Vecchio* is less acidic in taste and leans toward the sweeter side, thus making it a great dessert condiment. It can be drizzled over fine Parmigiana Reggiano, strawberries or vanilla ice cream, whereas the younger kinds of vinegar, being more assertive (as is the case with wine), are more conducive to use over meats and other main courses (*secondi*). It can be sipped straight after dinner as a *digestivo*. A good reference source is <u>The Balsamic Vinegar</u>

Cookbook, by Meesha Halm, published by Collins Publishers of San Francisco.

So, kick back with your favorite *Balsamico Tradizionale*, grab a cordial glass and a hunk of *Parmigiana Reggiano*, then slip back to the Emilia Romagna of a hundred years ago. It might not hurt to pull out a twenty-year-old *Amarone Classico della Valpolicella* to help you forget the two hundred bucks that vile of vinegar set you back.

Some Culinary Travel Suggestions

There are many more interesting and important regions of the world not included here. This is not due to quality or importance, but that those identified below are some of the places that Joanne and I have visited.

Cultural differences

As is the case with terroir, so it is with cultural characteristics. Let us break it down into two very broad categories: US or California (Australia, some

South American, Spain in the case of Ribera del Duero) and European (Chile and Argentina).

It is no secret that California's climate is characterized by long, hot growing seasons. That means more juice with more sugar to be converted to more alcohol. In addition, many of them, both red and white, spend a great deal of time in oak. The result is bigger, upfront, highly tannic wines that are not shy about introducing themselves to you and telling you everything about them in an instant. At times, they can dominate the conversation. They are beautiful and uniquely characteristic. This is one reason why they were able to be a major player in the world market so quickly.

The European wines are quite different. They are more subtle, they need some time to reveal themselves and as complex as they can be, they almost never dominate the conversation. In general, they can be slightly lower in alcohol, a bit more subtle and, though vibrant participants, almost never dominate the conversation. What they may not manifest up front is made up for in complexity, style and grace. They, too, are beautiful and uniquely characteristic. You can pick your favorite, or simply enjoy both in the proper context, as I have for decades. As I stated earlier, my personal standard was set by Bordeaux.

Tuscany

This is arguably one of the most romanticized regions of the world, not only for its geographic splendor, but for its complex political and rich artistic and culinary history. Using Siena as your base, if you can, try to visit the three most important towns of the *Chianti Region*: *Greve*, *Radda* and *Castellina*. Not far away is the towered town of *San Gimignano*, a must-see destination. Two other important wine areas are *Montalcino*, home of the fabled *Brunello di Montalcino* and *Montepulciano,* source of the famed *Vino Nobile di Montepulciano* (not to be confused with *Montepulciano d'Abruzzo,* a totally different wine and region).

Sanguis Jovis, The Blood of Jupiter, the Heart of Tuscany,

A closer look at Sangiovese

When admiring the great wines of the world, you can't help but wonder just what makes them great. Could it be the species, the quality of the grape, the handling of the grapes at harvest, the vinification or ageing process? The answer to all of these is a resounding, "Yes!" But it all starts with the grape. Let's take a close look at *Sangiovese,* the grape that is the primary component of two of the world's great wines: *Chianti* and those known as *Super Tuscans.*

The Sangiovese is a versatile grape that acquired its name from the Etruscans. This deep, red berry was known to them as Sanguis Jovis or the blood of Jupiter. The grape is now grown in many parts of the world, but its unquestioned homeland is Italy, primarily Tuscany and surrounding regions. The Italians refer to two types of Sangiovese, the *Sangiovese Grosso* (big) and *Sangiovese Piccolo* (small), but it's not that simple. In this case, the *grosso* refers to the smaller grape and vice versa. *Grosso*, in this case indicates importance and quality, i.e., the smaller grape produces the best wines and is therefore, bigger in importance. Like many varieties, the Sangiovese takes on a different character wherever it's grown and each district in Italy has a different name for the same grape. In *Scansano*, it's called *Morellino (Morellino di Scansano)*, in *Montepulciano*, it's *Prugnolo Gentile*, in *Montalcino*, it's *Brunello*, etc.

This small grape (the grosso) produces Bordeaux-style wines that are rich, intensely extracted and colored, and can vary from medium to full body with an alcohol content of 12.5 – 14.5 %. Its diminutive size means that there is a higher percentage of skin relative to its total mass. Since the skin (stem and seed) is where the tannins come from, many of these wines are predisposed to ageing in the bottle for years if not decades.

In the seven districts of Chianti in the heart of Tuscany (*Chianti, Chianti Classico, Colli Fiorentini, Colli Senesi, Colli Aretini, Montalbano and Rufina*), the wines vary greatly in style due to the terroir, or influence of the location, soil, climate, exposure, etc. The further west of Florence, the lighter, fresher and fruitier the wine. The further east of Florence toward Rufina, the wines are full-bodied and capable of improving for decades, particularly in great vintages such as 1997, 2015, 2016 and 2019.

As you proceed south to Montalcino, a magnificent town that sits at a lower altitude and has a warmer microclimate, the growing season becomes longer. As a result, the grapes ripen longer taking on a brownish hue, hence the name Brunello. Don't forget that a longer, warmer growing season means more sugar in the grapes to be converted to alcohol during the fermentation process. That's one reason why Brunello di Montalcino is such a big and luscious wine.

So, what does all of this mean to you, the consumer? It means great wines and an exciting world of wines of various styles, weights and prices. Remember that Italy, like France, has strict laws governing the origins and processing of grapes. A wine cannot be called Chianti unless the Sangiovese grapes are grown, and the wine is produced right in the Chianti district. It must also be comprised of no more than 90% Sangiovese; the balance can now be a few other varieties such as *Caniaolo Nero, Merlot,* etc. If a wine is made from 100% Sangiovese, which many fine makers are now producing, the wine cannot be called Chianti and it cannot even carry a D.O.C.G. designation (Denominazione d'Origine Controllata e Guarantita). It must carry the I.G.T. designation (Indicazione Geografica Tipica). This is the designation that almost all the Super Tuscans carry. Since most Super Tuscans are a single variety or a blend that is not governed, there is no other legal designation for them. In the case of Chianti Classico, ageing is even controlled. To be called a *Riserva,* the wines must age in oak for 39 months after which, if it is not deemed ready by the *Consorzio,* it must undergo additional ageing in three-month increments only prior to bottling, then another year in the bottle before release. You can see why some of these wonderful wines are so expensive. BTW, if you want real value in

Sangiovese, look for one produced from outside of Tuscany, perhaps neighboring *Umbria* and *Emilia-Romagna*.

Generally, Sangiovese produces a wine with a characteristic *"Barnyard"* essence on the nose, most notably just as the bottle is opened. There is also a slight bitterness on the back of the palate. It is definitely a "food wine" meaning that it tastes rounder and more balanced when accompanied by food flavors such as roasted meat or game. Many Sangiovesi are characterized by a certain obvious acidity that enables them to accompany tomato-based sauces and dishes as well. This is why it is a variety that has enjoyed huge success by being blended with rounder varieties such as Merlot and Canaiolo.

Whether you want a pleasant patio wine with your pizza, a Vino Nobile di Montepulciano with your

Salsiccia di Cinghiale or a Brunello di Montalcino with your wood-oven roasted pheasant, Sangiovese covers the entire spectrum for you in grand style. It is also a very reliable red with seafood. So, grab a glass and visit Tuscany right in your own kitchen.

The Abbey of Good Harvests

A special visit to Tuscany's Badia a Coltibuono

The day was sun-drenched and deceptively cool. A brilliant, azure sky dotted with creampuff clouds served as the backdrop for dramatic hills laced in vines, highlighted by meticulous olive groves and outlined by serpentine dirt roads lined with tall cypress trees. Save the temperature, this was a classic day in the Chianti region of Tuscany. Tempted as we were to sit on the terrace of our hotel on the outskirts of Siena and wax poetically, a full day of work was ahead of us – *hard* work. The plan was to drive those cypress-lined roads up the mountain for a 4:00 pm appointment at a very special place to taste some of the finest wine and olive oil in the world. On the way, a stop at the classic Chianti towns of Radda and Castellina in Chianti and a meeting with Salvatore Mantelli of the noted *Dievole* winery – with a tasting, of course!

The destination was *Badia a Coltibuono* (Abbey of Good Harvests), founded by Benedictine monks in 1051. The Abbey has been a center of wine production for a thousand years. Most recently (only a mere two hundred years), the estate has been in the nurturing hands of the Stucchi-Prinetti family who acquired it from Napoleon (not much history here!). Let us now turn to a forty-year-old movement, *"agritourismo"*. Well, Pietro Stucchi-Prinetti was the first in the Chianti area to welcome tourists to his property as students of the Tuscan culinary tradition. His wife, Lorenza de 'Medici, established the cooking school some fifty years ago, and it's now one of the hottest culinary destinations in Europe.

We were met at the premises by the most gracious and charming, Dr. Cristina Biagini. After a tour of the fifteenth century building complex: the Abbey, a courtyard around an ancient well, the gardens, the private wine cellars, the ageing cellars, the refectory and the restaurant, the kind Dr. escorted us through a small doorway and up a stairway to the private tasting room. This was not a room for lavish feasts, but rather a large, well-appointed room that exuded enough history and tradition, but most of all, a room with a purpose – the serious evaluation of the estate's product line: wine, olive oil, grappa, honey and balsamic vinegar. (We have been intimately familiar with the Badia a Coltibuono wines and oils for many years. The first serious Chianti we ever acquired back in 1976 was from this estate and we have been drinking Coltibuono wines ever since. The olive oils are equally integral in our home.) Cristina pulled out a wine that we were NOT familiar with – their '97 *Sangioveto*. This is NOT a Chianti, in fact, like many of the "Super Tuscans" it can't even carry the D.O.C.G. (Denominazione d'Origine Controllata e Guarantita) designation but rather, the I.G.T. (Indicazione Geografica Tipica) which is common to most Super Tuscans and non-classified blends. Its composition is 100% Sangioveto. She opened the bottle and proceeded to 'season' the glasses by pouring about an ounce into one glass then, swirling it to completely coat the inside of the bowl, then finally poured its contents into another glass to repeat the procedure, etc.

The moment it was poured, you could see that it was "serious" wine. It was so concentrated and extracted – loaded with glycerin (beautiful, long, slow, legs) and a ripe, fruity aroma. The grapes come from older vines (low yields and high concentration). The wine spends about three weeks in contact with the skins and is then aged in *French Allier Oak barriques* for a year, after which the wine ages an additional year in the bottle prior to its limited release. The wine was stunning, a bit young at that point – full of tannins, fruit and very assertive, but with the requisite 'bones and stuff' to cellar for many, many years. It is truly a reserve wine. The 2015 should command a price of about $70.00 a bottle – well worth it if you like fine, old Sangiovese wines after they've been cellared for years and years.

Next, she brought out some Tuscan bread (no salt, no seeds) and olive oils. These aren't oils for cooking. They are oils to be unaltered by heat and to be used as condiments, i.e., drizzled on the food just prior to being served. The Extra Virgin Olive Oil comes from orchards replanted after the devastating frost of 1985. It is expensive, about $60.00 for 750 ml bottle but if used as a condiment, it should last a few weeks (much longer than a bottle of wine at that or any price!) Their *Albereto Extra Virgin Olive Oil* is made in limited quantities with olives grown exclusively on their *Podere Albereto* orchard, handpicked, cold pressed and unfiltered. This oil sells for about $55.00 for a 500mm bottle – an oil to be used discreetly! These oils are very low in acidity and though light, possess a concentrated flavor. Both oils should be consumed within eighteen months of release to really show their freshness. Another fine oil is their *Campo Corto*, "*da agricoltura biologica*" (organic), made exclusively from the *Frantoio* variety of olives. The olives are pressed on the same day of the harvest. The oil is unfiltered and somewhat cloudy, but in time, it clears completely. It has an intense, grassy aroma with hints of artichoke and aromatic herbs. The flavor is intense and vibrant, and the aftertaste is peppery. It commands a slightly higher price than the Albereto. All of these oils are now classified as "organic".

After our tastings, Dr. Biagini escorted us to their restaurant run by one of the Stucchi-Prinetti sons and we dined on the mountaintop under the Tuscan moonlight. As luck would have it, we were able to order a bottle of an older Sangioveto with dinner. That wine developed into a hearty – robust wine and the three years of additional age made a huge difference in terms of harmony and complexity. We were fortunate to have this *"mini vertical tasting"* (same wine, diff vintages) of this great, single variety, single estate wine. The dinner itself was a multi-course feast, simple in its indigenous fare and presentation, but apocalyptic in the quality, intensity, and harmony of the ingredients. Now we are certain where the name of the estate comes from. This was a workday not soon to be forgotten.

Fattoria Colle Verde

Lucca, the gorgeous walled city, the birthplace of legendary composers like Giacomo Puccini and Luigi Boccherini, is a must-stop if you are anywhere near this part of Tuscany. We paid a visit not many years ago and delighted in walking the Passeggiata atop the walls surrounding the city. While there, we had arranged to meet Piero Tartagni, acclaimed film producer turned winemaker, olive oil producer and manager of the Fattoria Colle Verde, a wonderful estate which is now an agritourismo destination. He is one of those creative, ultra-passionate folks I referred to earlier. Piero spent an entire afternoon with us, guiding us around the beautiful property. As it turns out, he is a sophisticated music lover and much to our surprise, he knew and actually hosted the late Argentine tango legend, Astor Piazzolla, whose music we recorded and have performed for decades.

We have visited many estates and winemakers, but this was our first, hands-on look at actual olive oil production, oils of the highest quality, unmistakably evident by the aromas in the air as soon as we approached the site of processing, quite remarkable and unforgettable.

Tuscany is the birthplace of the *"Super Tuscan"* wines. Ironically, they carry the highest price tags and the lowest legal classification of I. G. T. because their blend is a *Bordeaux* style blend that does not adhere to the Italian legal requisites of the region. The first of the great Super Tuscans were the *"Tigs and Aias"*: *Tignalello* and *Solaia* (produced by *Antinori*), *Ornellaia* and *Sassicaia*. These are exquisite wines, well worth the price, primarily made from cabernet sauvignon and cabernet franc, with some merlot and petit syrah in some cases. This trip, for us, was a gem.

We find that the wines of Italy reflect the nature of the natives, as they are from the first sniff, *"accogliernte"*, welcoming.

Italy North, Piemonte and Verona

Slow food, Barbaresco and Shakespeare! What can be better?

Let's begin our journey in the foothills of the Alps, Piemonte – one of the most dramatic geographical regions on earth. This is a land of rugged mountains, extreme swings in weather and the perfect environment for one of the finickiest grape varieties known to man, *Nebbiolo*. In many respects, this variety is similar in personality and attitude to *Pinot Noir*. It is found only in specific microclimates and it either thrives or dies. It is the predominant grape of the region, growing alongside *Barbera*, *Cortese* and others.

The three main locales are *Alba*, the home of the *Slow Food* movement, *Barolo* and *Barbaresco*, nestled in the *Langhe Hills*. The Nebbiolo grape derived its name from the Italian word, "*nebbia*" or fog. The grapes cling low to the vines of the dense, fog-laden vineyards. The wines are highly structured, delicious, and capable of ageing in good vintages. Due to the terroir, they are a fabulous accompaniment to foods with mushrooms and truffles, slow-roasted meats and risotto.

The perfect Nebbiolo feast:
Stuffed portabella mushrooms and osso buco.

Now, we venture a little further southeast to the enchanting and exciting city of Verona. This bustling city is so much fun on so many levels. You have the ancient Arena di Verona (an outdoor theater from Roman times still in vibrant use during the summer Opera Season), the Centro Storico, the home of Romeo Montague and many more interesting sites. Verona is also the gateway to *Valpolicella*, the glorious wine region that produces the coveted *Amarone* and the *Valpolicella Classico* wines. The producers to visit here are *Tommasi, Allegrini, Nando, Santi* and *Masi.*

The principal grapes are the *Corvina, Rondinella* and *Molinara*, all three in the legal mix for the extraordinarily rich Amarone.

*Staging for Verdi's "Aida" in
the Arena di Verona*

Corvina grapes ripening in

Valpolicella.

Of special note is the production process for Amarone. The three grape varieties are harvested, laid out on rakes to dry for several months, THEN, the raisins are crushed, making for a very, rich wine. The left-over skins and stems are preserved to be used by passing ordinary Valpolicella wine through them to extract the character of Amarone. This method is called *Ripasso*, and the wines are often referred to as *Baby Amarone*. Amarone itself is so rich that it can accompany a full-bodied meal as well as many desserts, such as Pears Poached in Amarone, ummmmmm!

Champagne

Le Collier de Perles

The Collar of Pearls

Champagne and a Toast to Life!

A friend once commented that, "Yanni is one of the most phenomenal classical musicians on the scene." When I queried as to why he thought Yanni was a "classical" musician, he stated, "There are violins in his orchestra." Well, violins do not a symphony make, nor bubbles a Champagne.

A magnum of fine Champagne, a celebration…
I don't remember what we were celebrating!
But it must have been important!

To many, Champagne is a bubbly, fruity, white wine, semi-sweet if not sweet and an icon of celebration. This lively, fruity and at times spicey and acidic wine can be reminiscent of green apples, pears, sometimes lemon or citrus, other times, nuts and honey, but is always predisposed to yeast and toast. The term itself needs some definition if we're to truly appreciate what this wonder of northern French viticulture has to offer. Most wines are categorized as either regional wines, named for the region of origin or varietal wines, named for the grape variety. Champagne is a district in France, seventy-five miles east of Paris, embracing the noted cities of Épernay, Ay, Marne and Reims. Hence, the term "Champagne" refers to a regional wine. French law is very explicit and strict in this matter with its *Appellation Controllée* designations. Only a wine produced in the very district of Champagne, in the strict *Methóde Champenoise,* using a specific blend of grapes grown in

Champagne can carry the *"Champagne" Appellation Controllée.* A wine originating close to but not precisely from Champagne must be called *Charmant.* French law, however, has no muscle or authority outside of France, so the world uses the term loosely, if not universally, for most bubbly wines.

It may be useful to examine the wine and its evolution before we discuss its context at or around the table. Champagne started out as a still, red wine. Hailing from the North of France, where seasonal differences in daily temperature are huge, the fermentation process can be tricky. After the harvest in late September/early October, fermentation begins as temperatures are still warm enough to be catalytic to the process. In times prior to climate control, fermentation would cease when temperatures would drop through November whether or not all of the sugar in the wine had converted to alcohol. The wine was then bottled, BUT, as temperatures rose again in the spring, the bottled wine would begin to ferment a second time, this time, in the bottle, creating Carbon Dioxide in the wine, the source of the bubbles. Though this process has been attributed to the celebrated Benedictine monk of the early 18th century, *Dom Pérignon*, the process was well underway prior to his historic predawn exclamation, "Come quickly! I'm tasting stars!" This secondary fermentation in the bottle is known as the *Methóde Champenoise* and is the only generally accepted method for producing quality sparkling wine wherever it is produced. There is a much cheaper method known as the *"Cuvée Close"* in which the secondary fermentation takes place in large, hermetically sealed, stainless-steel vats prior to bottling. This is common in many *Spanish Cava* wines, some *Prosecco* wines of Italy and several sparkling California wines.

Another complicated procedure in the Methóde Champenoise is the *"de gorgement"* or removal of the sediment during the process. This technique was developed by the most famous lady in the storied history of Champagne, *Madame* or *Veuve Clicquot-Ponsardin* (the Widow Clicquot). Removing the sediment from the bottles after winter hibernation was a challenge but she discovered that storing the bottles upside down and turning them periodically would cause the sediment to collect and form a cap in the neck of the bottle. After the wine was sufficiently clear, she ran the necks of the upside-down bottles through ice water to freeze the cap. With a quick shake of the bottle, the cork was removed, the gas would force out the cap and the bottle would then be immediately stopped with a cork and a wire basket. *Voilá, le "degorgement!* Some wine is lost in the process, however, so it is replaced by a juice of varying sugar content to create a wine of the desired sweetness, i.e., *Brut, Extra Dry*, etc.

While on the topic of fermentation, we can't avoid touching upon the degree of sweetness in the wine from Brut to Extra Dry, to Sweet. The amount of residual sugar that is left in the blend will dictate the level of sweetness. Most fine Champagnes are Brut (very dry). Extra Dry is actually (semi-dry) and Rosé is nothing more than a wine that has remained in contact with the red grapes skins in the must long enough to add just the right amount of color. Let's not forget the *Blanc de Noirs* (white wine from black grapes). This wine is made mostly from *Pinot Noir,* but the skins have been removed before they impart any pigment to the must or juice. *Blanc de Blancs* is made solely from white grapes, almost always Chardonnay.

There is no other beverage more closely associated with celebration than Champagne. It is the ultimate "toast". Whether it's a $12.00 Korbel from Napa Valley or a *Vintage "La Grande Dame", Veuve Clicquot-Ponsardin*, the message is still the same – it's time to celebrate! Having said that, we must mention that the French take their Champagne very seriously. In fact, in addition to the laws governing the appellation, they also have laws that specifically define the texture and bubbles in it. Carbonation is what gives Champagne its life. Without it, it would be a still, white wine. The bubbles are the first visual contact with wine after it is poured. That wondrous cap of bubbles that immediately forms at the top of the glass is referred to as, *"le collier des perles"* or the collar of pearls. The bubbles are measured in units of air pressure known as *atmospheres*. A Champagne with 4 –6 atmospheres of pressure is called *moeussaux* (thick and frothy like mousse), 2 – 4 atmospheres is *crémant*, less than two is *petillant*, and slightly fizzy is *frizzante*. The bubbles in Champagne make it a most versatile drink that can stand well enough on its own, yet a wonderful accompaniment to just about any dish. It is particularly good with shellfish and really shows its stuff around foods prepared with fermented condiments such as Japanese soya, miso, wasabi and sashimi. The yeasty overtones are a perfect match.

Oh, the grapes! What about the grapes used in making this extraordinary wine? Well, Champagne, as you know, is usually a blend, not only of grapes but of vintages. That's why there is such consistency of style from each producer. Only in great vintages will a Champagne be produced from grapes of only that vintage and sold as a *"single vintage"* Champagne.

A recent visit to the Champagne region provided us with an opportunity to explore the two main cities of Champagne in detail. The first was *Reims*, the second, *Épernay*. What an unforgettable trip. Between the two towns, we visited Veuve Clicquot Ponsardin, Mumm, Taittinger, Moët et Chandon (producers of Dom Pérignon), Domaine Pommery, Nicolas Feuillat and several smaller, less known, but nonetheless high-quality producers.

A tasting at the influential Domaine Pommery, Reims, France

The grapes are a blend of *Pinot Noir* (red grape), *Chardonnay*, and *Petit Meunier*. New York State wineries, particularly in the beautiful Finger Lakes region, usually use the native *Delaware* grape in their "Champagnes"; however, *Dr. Konstantin Frank's* Chateau Frank is producing a wonderful Methóde Champenoise from the classic Burgundian grape blend with those same *vinifera* varieties grown in New York State (*Ch. Frank Brut*).

So, are you having an ordinary day, if not worse? Lighten it up with a pop of the cork, some bubbles and a delectable drink – you can't help but smile.

Bordeaux

Classic beyond Classic!

I am often asked, "Michael, if there were only one wine on earth that you had to drink, what wine would it be?" My immediate response is, "Bordeaux!" No thought required here. As I mentioned earlier in this writing, Bordeaux is the wine that set the bar for me early on in my Sedimental Journey. It is a true classic.

The principal grapes of the region are cabernet sauvignon and merlot, depending on which part of Bordeaux you happen to be in.

In the Medoc, the blend is based upon cabernet sauvignon with a mix of merlot, cabernet franc, malbec and petit verdot. In St. Emilion and Graves, it is reversed. The blend here is merlot based with cabernet sauvignon in the same mix as the rest. These are all highly prized wines capable of tremendous age and improvement, yielding unspeakable complexity. The city of Bordeaux is lovely and a visit to the village of St. Emilion will stay with you a lifetime

Château Haut-Bailly, Pessac-Léognan

A history and a circle of personal friends

Shortly before a concert tour of southern France, some dear friends who were part of a large wine-loving group of wine and food lovers introduced us to Larry Draves and his friend and partner, the late Meg Summersgill. Small world indeed as Larry was a banker and close assistant to the late Robert Wilmers, former President and CEO of M and T Bank. In 1998, Wilmers and his French wife, Elizabeth, acquired Château Haut-Bailly from the famed Sanders family, who made this estate a fixture in Bordeaux history. Wilmers restored the property and level of vinification with the assistance of Véronique Sanders. Wilmers asked Larry and Meg if they would be interested in assisting at the property in various management roles: Meg was a retired French professor and culinary sophisticate, so it was perfect.

Larry and Meg knew of our imminent tour and invited us to be guests at the Chateaux, an offer one could not refuse. We spent five days there, rehearsing and performing at other properties in the area and it was truly magical. The irony is that Ch. Haut-Bailly was one of the first wines, along with Ch. D'Agassac, that I started to collect and drink for decades. I am still holding a bottle of the 1998 for reasons of history and posterity, but also have cases of several great vintages in the cellar. Their second label, *Le Parde de Haut-Bailly* is well worth experiencing, particularly in great vintages.

Burgundy

Noble beyond Noble

The iconic and historic Hospice de Beaune

The wines of Burgundy are among the most sought-after in the world and for good reason. They have a long history and tradition of quality defined by sheer elegance. This is in no small part due to the dominant grape variety, the beloved *Pinot Noir*. Unlike the Cabernet Sauvignon that can grow virtually anywhere (hence the name: sauvignon, which means wild), the Pinot Noir is a finicky grape, very sensitive to soil and climate conditions. Here, the estates are referred to as Domains, rather than Châteaux. One of the most expensive wines on earth, *Domaine de la Romanée-Conti,* is produced here.

Chablis and shrimp cocktail!

As for fabled white wines, this area is also legendary. *Puligny Montrachet, Pouilly-Fuissé* and *Chablis* are just some of the most familiar names of these extraordinary wines. These are Chardonnay-based wines with less manipulation than their California counterparts, i.e., less wood and less *malolactic fermentation.* Speaking of terroir, the village of *Chablis* hosts chalky soil and is situated over a bedrock vein consisting of Kimmeridgian Limestone, a former seabed loaded with fossilized shellfish, i.e., oysters, clams, shrimp, etc. If you want to experience a truly glorious wine and food combo, try a shrimp, scallop and crab ceviche with a fine bottle of Chablis. If you have not yet embraced the concept of terroir, this will surely do it for you.

The specific region is the *Côtes de Beaune,* an enchanting and lovely area.

The Rhône Valley

Opulence from the Get-go with the appropriate Infallibility!

If you want to get someone's attention with a gift bottle of wine, give them a Rhône wine. Even the least expensive will immediately greet you with a welcoming bouquet. These are opulent wines at every level and why not? This region was sought-after by the Papacy and Conclave of Cardinal from 1309 to 1376. *Châteauneuf-du-Pape* is the commune of the luscious wine of the same name (the nine chateaux of the Pope). The fragrant complexity is derived from the blend, which can legally include thirteen varieties of grape, the principal ones being *Mourvèdre, Cinsault, Syrah* and *Grenache*. Many great wines come from the region. You will see names such as *Gigondas, Vacqueyras, Côtes du Rhône* and many others.

One of my favorites from the northern Rhône Valley is *Crozes-Hermitage*, a full, somewhat smoky and delicious wine that is very popular and versatile.

The main target destinations here are *Avignon, Aix-en-Provence* and of course, *Marseille*.

Spain and Portugal

Vino, Sherry, Porto, Flamenco and Fado

The Iberian Peninsula is, without a doubt, one of the most dramatic and diverse geographic areas on earth, with a huge variety of wines and micro-cultures. What Sangiovese is to Tuscany, *Tempranillo* is to Spain and particularly *Rioja*, the most popular wine region of Spain. A plethora of grape varieties thrive here but none more so than Tempranillo. The wines of this territory traditionally have been more Bordeaux-style, unlike their counterparts a little further north near *Valladolid*, the *Ribera del Duero*. In the Ribera, the wines lean more toward the California style in structure and appearance. One of the world's most sought-after wines is the expensive, unique and heralded *Vega Sicilia*.

Further south, the miles upon miles of olive trees in *Andalucía* construct a unique terroir in the wines here. Many wonderful whites flourish here as throughout Spain. Look for *Albariño*, a most pleasant summer, patio wine. The same grape is used in Portugal to produce *Vinho Verde*, the sparkling counterpart!

Two of the other wonderful regions of Iberia are *Jerez* and *Porto*. Jerez is the home of *Sherry*, and *Porto*, of course, Port wine, two fortified wines that have been cornerstones of literary traditions for countless decades. An item for everyone's bucket list is a daylong boat trip up the *Douro River* from Porto in Portugal.

California Wine Country

From gold to silicon to wine.

Though slightly further south in latitude and a bit longer, California is situated much like Italy, even close to the same geographic angle. It is agriculturally, culturally and artistically rich and diverse. The seductive North California wine country is divided by the glorious *Mayacamas Mountains* with *Sonoma* to the west and *Napa Valley* to the east, each producing world-class wines, red and white, sparkling and still. To the south, the two areas meet up in *Carneros (Domain Carneros – Taittinger)*. An absolute must-visit is to the exquisite and elegant Domaine Carneros, a property of the renowned Champagne producer, Taittinger. This will be an unforgettable experience – be sure to try their tasting featuring some delightful sparkling wines...and oysters!

Due to the fabulous climate, California boasts long, hot growing seasons that produce fruit high in juice and sugar. That means they are higher in alcohol. The white wines are beautiful chardonnays that typically spend more time in oak than their European counterparts and tend to be more crafted by malolactic fermentation and longer exposure to oak, as we discussed earlier.

The reds are big, rich, strong and in many cases, extremely complex (and expensive). This is a truly memorable tourist destination, so be sure you spend a bit of time here.

SUMMARY

Nothing stays the same. Since I began collecting wine decades ago, the world and the wines have changed dramatically due to many factors, not the least of which are globalization and climate change: audacious blends – world market, high alcohol, champagne style wines from the UK, unheard of twenty-five years ago.

We have come to the point where you have done everything that a *wine connoisseur* does, just not as often perhaps – not to mention that you aren't getting paid for it! All that you need to do now is repeat the process over and over again. I appreciate the fact that this is a tough assignment, but it will reward you time and time again. You may even find, as I did, that even though the wine experience is a greater part of your life, you will probably be consuming less quantities of wine just because you are spending more time with each drop, instead of just swallowing mouthfuls of this glorious beverage.

SAVOR THE MOMENT!!! It is my sincere hope that you now have a better *"practical"* understanding of why wine has been such a cherished and revered commodity for over five thousand years. If you take the steps I have outlined, I'll bet that you will never forget the wine you sampled on the very first step you took with me on this fantastic journey through the world of wine. Eat, drink and live wisely. Be passionate about your wine and you will be passionate about your life.

Share it all in great health and prosperity with all of

those you love as well as those you don't. We will

all be much happier.

Well, that was awesome! Our time together has passed. Here I sit in Sorrento, with a delightfully empty glass and Mt. Vesuvius over my shoulder. What could be better? Thank you for your company! You know that I will remember every moment. And these are... My Sediments, Exactly!

Joanne and I wish you well.

Cin, Cin!!!

Reminder ~ Never drink before driving!

www.castellaniandriaccio.com

ABOUT THE AUTHORS

The Castellani Andriaccio Duo in Concert
With the Buffalo Philharmonic Orchestra
Photo credit: The Buffalo News

Award-winning international touring and recording artists, Joanne Castellani and Michael Andriaccio have enjoyed a celebrated career as one of the foremost and most important classical guitar duos in history. Recognized as the pre-eminent American Guitar Duo, the nation's capital has embraced them with two National Endowment for the Arts Solo Recitalist Fellowships. They have been featured in concert at the White House, the Smithsonian Institution, and the JFK Center for the Performing Arts and have been consultants to the Music Division of the Library of Congress. In addition, they are members of the Alice Tully Circle of the Chamber Music Society of Lincoln Center. The Duo has recorded ten acclaimed cds, two named "Best of the Year" by Fanfare Magazine and American Record Guide. Critics around the globe, from the New York Times to Gramophone Magazine, have unanimously praised their *"elegance, style, poise and exquisite taste in interpretation"*. For more information on their musical activities and legacy, please visit www.castellaniandriaccio.com.

Their passion for the arts and all good things in life has enabled them to seize touring opportunities to experience some of the greatest culinary locations in the world, and to meet some of the people who are driving forces in this realm. Joanne is a Certified Olive Oil Consultant (The Italian Culinary Institute in Manhattan) and Michael is a passionate wine lover, collector and painter. The two have lectured on wine and oil at Brock University, Niagara University School of Hospitality and Tourism, The Erie County Community College Culinary School, the Tops Cooking School and the Finger Lakes Wine Festival. They have also written numerous articles on the subject.

www.ingramcontent.com/pod-product-compliance
Lightning Source LLC
Chambersburg PA
CBHW051044050726
47592CB00002B/386